KOBIETY

(WOMEN)

A Novel of Polish Life

BY

SOFJA RYGIER-NALKOWSKA

TRANSLATED FROM THE POLISH

BY

MICHAEL HENRY DZIEWICKI

G. P. PUTNAM'S SONS

NEW YORK AND LONDON

The Knickerbocker Press

1920

CONTENTS

KOBIETY

KOBIETY

I

ICE-PLAINS

GIRT with a girdle of morning-glory and vetches in full blossom, and twining a great wreath of heavy corn-flowers round my head, I lie upon my back in the forest glade.

It is a fine summer afternoon, and sultry. In the pines overhead there is a faint murmur, continuous, a little sad; the birches, with their slender waving boughs, utter a quiet whisper, but no breeze is to be felt.

As I lie here, I presently fall to crooning a sing-song chant—not any known air, but one made up of many tunes, heard long ago, or never heard at all. The words, too, are either remembered, or they spring up as I sing. If the rhyme fails me, I do not break off the tune to find one, but make an assonance do just as well. So I sing of a dream I have dreamt, and then of love—hot, burning love,—and I end with an invocation to the Faun of the wood; for my desire is toward him.

It is warm and still. By fits and starts birds chirp—so softly that they seem to be whispering. I half expect to see a chamois, with long horns curling back from its brow, peep out wistfully from between the birch-trunks.

The sun, shining athwart the leaves that quiver, flings mobile twinkling rounds of light upon the pine-needles. I close my eyes. A great bright stain appears, followed by a succession of rainbow hues, ending in a spot of scarlet flame.

It is warm and still. The scent of wild thyme is in my nostrils. Behold me, a woodland nymph, awaiting the Faun of the woods!

I have left my vast ice-plains, my Northern Lights, my cold silvery dreams among the stalactites of my grottoes, and have come to bask in the strong sunshine of life.

And I welcome life with a peal of laughter, the outcome of many a day of tortured thought and fruitless pondering. I yield myself up to it, not from any internal weakness, but submitting to its brutality with a supreme effort that crushes down all repulsion, all revolt.

Upon the ruins of my mystic dreams there has grown up a lush rank flower—the worship of Life and its delights.

And my resignation is ungrudging, royally complete: for I do love life, in spite of all.

My mind—my cruel, insatiable, gloomy mind—would have put happiness to death; but I now trample it down. To-day I will pluck the flame-red blossom of Life: and my song shall call upon the Faun!

No Faun comes to my call; but instead of his hoofs, I hear the gallop of a horse in the distance. Laying my ear to the ground, I make sure.

Yes, I know: it is Janusz, coming after me. So I cease from singing, and lie silent and without motion; he is riding along the forest pathway, and I hope he may miss me, hidden here among the pines. And yet I am not unaware that, should he ride past and not discover me, I should feel disappointed. Notwithstanding, I make no movement. The only deceit I care to shun is self-deceit.

Janusz, who has seen me afar amongst the birches and the pines, urges his horse forward, and approaches behind me, so that I cannot catch sight of him. He means (so I guess) to come upon me suddenly with a rush, and frighten or flutter me, or in some way or other throw me off my balance. On which account, I take care not to make the least movement, lying with my hands clasped underneath my head, and looking up at the sky.

He rides at me with a swift run, and reins in his horse only two paces away from me. He at once realizes that my attitude is a challenge; it annoys him. There is a pause. In order to make me turn my head in his direction, he keeps his horse standing in the same place: this is hard to do.

But I too remain motionless, repressing a desire to laugh. Janusz is, I know, too good a rider to let his beast tread upon me. I can hear it snorting impatiently, and its hoofs pawing the ground.

The flies in the wood torment it so much that presently it is unable to restrain itself, and frets forward a few paces, to my side. And so I can see Janusz. A handsome man, in a light-coloured jockey's cap, tight-fitting trousers, and long patent leather boots; just now so vexed that his nostrils are quivering.

Bowing stiffly, he takes his right foot out of the stirrup, and prepares to dismount.

"You might have failed to see me, and ridden farther. I thought you would," I remark, with a faint uninterested smile.

"As it happened, I did not fail."

"So I see."

"Did you want me to fail?"

"I did."

"For what reason, pray?"

"I was in a very pleasant mood—a sort of pantheistic mingling with Nature, that requires solitude to be enjoyed."

"All the same, I am going to stay," he says with a determined air, and carefully ties his horse's reins to a pine-branch.

A silence follows. Janusz brushes a few pine-cones out of his way, and then seats himself by my side. I sit up likewise, arrange the wreath of corn-flowers on my head, and lean back against a trunk.

"Do you not see that we are at odds?" he asks at length.

"That may very well be," I answer with some disdain. "And how did you find out where I was?"

"I followed you."

"Did you, indeed?"

"My balcony commands an extensive view. Your rose-coloured dress was plainly to be seen, as you went along the meadows and fields. You followed the path that skirts the ditch, did you not? And so on to the wood, where you disappeared. I followed on horse-back along the highroad: a far shorter way."

"Yes, your way; straight on, but less picturesque than mine."

"Am I to see some hidden meaning in this?"

"Oh, no, you need not—as you choose."

Janusz is of those who love "intellectual" talk; I put forth all the social tact that I have, and do my best to keep down to his level. I strive to attract him, not with my good looks, but with my mental charms, which I have now enlisted in the service of my physical self. My coquetry varies in quality as does the psychical character of its object; and thus it never fails in artistry. Here I am guided by the Law of Contrast. For instance, when I first flirted with Roslawski, I brought into play the primitive elemental sides of my nature; though indeed I had later to change all my tactics. And it is my quality as a woman—with my womanly wisdom and wit and originality—that I am acting upon Janusz; should I lose half my good looks, I should still, as a woman, be not less lovable in his eyes. In the psychology of contemporary love, this is a significant fact.

Over his handsome clean-cut face, a glow passes now and again. His eyes are fixed upon my features. I meanwhile, swift in change as a chameleon, and bright with radiant looks and glances, am watching him with artistic and quite impersonal interest: with those quivering sensitive nostrils, he makes me think of some beautiful high-bred animal. His eyes, which usually beam and glisten, are at preasent dimmed and glazed over, as if their fire had been extinguished, burned out by the passion within him. Now and then his eyes fall before mine, and he attempts to call up a pleasant smile; but in the attempt his white teeth glitter dangerously.

A gnat has settled on his forehead, and I tell him so. He waves it away listlessly.

"Let it bite," he says with a smile; "it matters little. I have blood enough and to spare."

There is a touch of self-satisfaction in his

voice as he says this. It was then a mistake of mine to have supposed him unaware of the nature of his strength. Knowledge of one's strong points makes for happiness; he is enviable.

Now he takes up some pine-cones, with which he pelts his horse playfully. It begins to kick and stamp. Instead of teasing the poor brute to no purpose, he ought (I say) to take one of the trees for his mark; and with that I go up to the horse. It gives me a distrustful look out of its beautiful eyes, while I stroke and pat its neck.

"Miss Janina, do not go so near my beast; it may hurt you."

"You were not afraid when it was but now standing close to my head," I reply laughingly.

"But I was holding it in then," he mutters between his set teeth.

Up he comes, stretching out his hand to pull me away by force; but I flash him a quick glance of surprise, and at once he is subdued.

"I beg you," he says in a voice half-strangled with emotion, "I beg you to let me kiss your hand."

He is quite close to me. One instant I am hot as fire; but I do not draw away from him, nor put my hands behind me. Standing motionless, with my half-averted head bent down close to the horse's mane, I answer calmly:

"I will not."

Janusz, with dog-like obedience, shrinks back, and stands a few paces away.

"Let us go home now," I say after a short silence; "but you must let me ride your horse."

"With the utmost pleasure; but then, how will you manage for a saddle?"

"Oh, that's all right. Even on your saddle, I can contrive to ride woman-fashion. Only you will have to arrange the stirrup."

I leap into the saddle, my foot just touching his hand. Janusz himself settles it in the stirrup, which he shortens for me. As he does so, I once more see a glow sweep over his face.

"Pray allow me to lead the horse. It is restive, and may throw you."

"No, thanks; I am not in the least afraid."

On a sudden, with an unexpected movement, he catches hold of me, and presses his face hard against my knees.

At the same instant nearly, I give the horse

a smart blow with my whip, and gallop away,
not looking behind me; it is not easy to keep
my balance on that saddle.

This I have done, not to escape from him,
nor as being in any sort of fear. It was only
that he should not perceive my flushed face—
flushed neither with indignation nor with
shame.

Janusz has gone to L. for some days. I am
alone with Martha, with whom I enjoy myself very much. There is no one else on earth
with whom I can share the delight of reading together wise and beautiful books. As
we read, we become lost in mutual admiration
at the depth and subtlety of the remarks we
make: whence arises a delightful state of
mind in which each loses consciousness of the
other being present. Our impressions are
equally instantaneous, equally immediate; a
look, a gesture, suffices for one to understand
the other. We are growing absolutely similar, all but identical. Set apart from all that
surrounds us, our minds meet on dizzy
heights, spanned by aërial bridges which
bring our souls together, over the tremendous
gulfs that stretch beneath us; thereon few can

walk, for the bridges are of gossamer threads. In the valleys of the mind it is not hard for two souls to come together; but as one reaches the mountain-tops, each is farther and farther apart, and the chasm between them becomes more and more profound; besides, at the tread of the first ponderous foot, those bridges of cunning workmanship, running from peak to peak, are broken and fall to pieces.

Nevertheless, there is no love, nor even much liking, between Martha and myself. We do not so much as call each other friends. We both agree that, between one woman and another, no true love is possible; and so we do not try to cheat ourselves with a counterfeit. But, though we do not say everything openly and in words, still we know and understand one another to perfection.

The one thing that could drive us apart would be mutual rivalry in love for a man. Happily, however, Martha holds this to be out of the question. Ascetically disposed, she prides herself on the fact that no one has ever loved her. She likes as a rule to play the part of one that the world and that men misunderstand and fail to appreciate. This part, moreover, she plays very gracefully, she being a pretty girl, and no one taking her too much in earnest.

"My life," she is wont to say, "is as pure as a blank page; no thrill is recorded there, no kiss, no blush. I have no faith save in this crystal transparency of my being; save in the knowledge that Life passes close to me, touches me, grazes me, and yet by some miracle never leaves upon my long white robe one streak from the golden pollen of the flowers she bears; no faith save in the immaculateness of this my soul, that can travel through a coal-mine, and yet come out white as snow. The only article of my faith, the sole thing I care for, is the conviction that I shall go through life nobly and beautifully, in sweetness and tranquillity infinite; that my passage upon earth will be all sunshine and loveliness: the blossoming of a rare and goodly flower. So may I die! Even though love could give me happiness, I still would stand aloof from it. . . ."

Yes, but now and then in the dim blue twilight, she plays *Der Frühling* of Grieg: and then I feel that what she says is not the truth. In her notes there is a tone of longing unspeakable, that begs, with gentle half-audible entreaty . . . for *something*. And that fair white soul of her is always sobbing with pain, and dreaming—ever dreaming—of love.

When all is said, I am clever, young, and good-looking: so I want to live my life. Nietzsche will not have us forget the law: *For a woman, a stick.* Amiel declares she must love one only, and obey a sex-morality that has been made for her alone. Garborg tells us that she ought not to go anywhere without a governess, so that her future husband may find suspicion impossible. In spite of all which, I am resolved to live my own woman's life.

Hitherto I have not found out what femininity essentially is. In the Roslawski period, I piously believed æsthetic feeling to be the great typical quality of womanliness. But now—Ellen Key asserts that the woman always shapes herself as the man desires. If then he, the Only One, be a primitive, masterful, despotic man, am I to season his siesta and cigar with witty conversation, and bind my hair and dance and sound the timbrel for him, whilst to all others my eyes alone are to be visible, my face hidden under a veil? I

want to live my woman's life . . . nothing
more. Until, perhaps . . .

Oh, how hard it is for a girl to bear, upon
her white and shapely shoulders, the awful
burden of conscious humanity!

At times, Janusz is as gentle as a tame
young wolf, and that ravenous look has faded
from his eyes. Then I permit him to kiss my
hands and lay them to his sunburnt cheeks.
When the wild beast within him has for a
while fallen asleep, he has all the kindness,
all the sweetness of a child. Yet even then I
feel the presence of a latent force which may
break out at any time: a force which—I cannot tell why—seems to me antagonistic.

"How I wish you would allow me to call
you my darling!" he said to-day, when sitting
at my feet on a bank of turf, and touching the
border of my skirt caressingly, like a favourite cat.

I looked from above at the long lashes of
his downcast eyes, at his scarlet lips, at his
beautifully chiselled nose, and said within
myself: "Why don't you then? I should
only just set one long loving kiss—two per-

haps—upon those lips of yours and leave you without one word of regret."

"Are you offended then?" he asked, looking up at me.

I knitted my brows slightly, but could not keep the corners of my mouth still.

"Yes, I am."

"But you are smiling. Why do you smile so strangely?"

And his eyes gaze at me from under his thick brows—gaze slyly and sweetly, while the hot blood burns in my cheeks. Never, in the days of Roslawski and our long-learned conversations about literature, did I feel such a sensation as this.

An evening party at the Sedniewski's, Topolow: somebody's name-day. All four of us go, Martha and I, the grandfather, and Janusz. Rather a large gathering: girls like flowers, fresh and bright-hued. Some of the young men have been brought for the occasion from as far as Lodz.

I go in, with my cheeks fresh and ruddy from our drive along the windy road: my dress is of a beautiful sea-green hue. The party is quaintly and prettily framed in a large low-ceilinged drawing-room, lighted from above by an antique chandelier, with tiers of branches that shed sparkling many-coloured light around. Along the walls stand many fine old pieces of furniture, and on the veranda outside an orchestra is softly tuning up.

As I enter, I make an impression—the usual one. For a time, whilst every glance is turned in my direction, I feel as if pitted against them all. But, though I scarce know any one here, I am not embarrassed even for one instant. The sensation of unfriendliness, borne in upon me from those around, the feeling of my loneliness in this throng, only produces in me a reaction of haughty defiance. I should feel more embarrassed if I did not make this impression, and should come in without attracting any attention at all.

As Madame Sedniewska welcomes me, I overhear a whispered remark on my left. "Dressed like a third-rate actress."

This interests me, and I turn round; for I think the observation, though quite beside the mark, rather neatly expressed. A tall girl, dressed in white, English style from head to foot, meets my eyes, and silently gives me back glance for glance. Beyond question it is she. After all the introductions have been made, I proceed by choice to converse with her.

Her name is Imszanska; she has an ugly *fiancé* and a handsome brother; the most interesting (I think) of all the young men present. He asks me politely how I like the country-side here, and then goes on talking to Martha, who in her evening dress looks less comely than her wont, her face being pale and wearing an expression of unnatural constraint.

We take tea; after which dancing begins.

Dancing is to me a pastime as pleasant as riding; and I dance splendidly. Again and again, in one of the long mirrors that reach to the floor, I see myself and the black arms which encircle me, my listless form thrown backwards indolently, sleepily as it were, my red lips contrasting with the white of my set teeth, and sea-green gauze floating round me in loose watery undulations; while about my figure twine the elastic snake-like stalks of great white nanuphar blossoms.

I am soon aware that I have made an impression—an impression so palpable that the women themselves pretend to be, not only unconcerned, but pleased at my success. One of them is so kind as to set a hairpin straight for me. At such an entertainment, the struggle to be first, though depriving it of some of the pleasure which it should directly give, affords us the interest of a game in which, the harder it is to win, the more intoxicating the victory becomes.

After the cotillon, which I danced with Imszanski, I stood up with Janusz for the "Oberek." He is a perfect master of ceremonies, and as such he is *sans peur et sans reproche.*

I like to dance with him most of all. He bears me along like a runaway steed. Careering in a tiny orbit, towards the centre of which we lean all the time, we turn round and round with vertiginous speed, like two planets run mad. Locked in each other's arms, carried onward by our own impetus, we glide along with half-closed eyes, involuntarily, all but unconsciously, with a passive motion, as if by ourselves unable to keep so tremendous a pace. Around us we perceive only a confused mass of thick clotted brightness; the lights, the mirrors, the brilliant circle of lookers-on, are no longer distinguishable as they fly round us: all is merged in one maze of colours.

A wild flame is gleaming in my partner's eyes, and their pupils are sparkling like sun-lit diamonds. Our maddening pace, together with that dancing tune, boisterous with its musically monotonous din, are acting upon him as a war-dance acts upon a primitive race.

As for me, though his hot breath is on me like a flame, I feel quite calm. Tired out, almost fainting, I meekly let his wild "rav-ishing strides" carry me along as he chooses.

At last I go back to my seat; a deafening thunder of applause greets us both; I bow my head to thank them, but can for some time distinguish nothing. Meanwhile I hear Janusz, who has regained his self-control, and is now ordering the orchestra to play the "Mazur."

Miss Imszanska, coming up and seating her-self by my side, says to me: "You dance with all the grace of a swan; my brother says he never saw anything like it."

In the intervals between the dances, we walk in the garden, which is extensive and full of trees. The white flowers of the to-bacco-plants, just visible at night against the blackness of the sward, breathe forth their strange and intense aroma. A sort of drowsy hallucination takes possession of me: I fancy I am on earth no longer, but in some Hades of flowers, of sweet sounds, of beautiful things, and of Night triumphant. I lean heavily on Janusz, almost nestling in his arms. My smile gleams white in the dusk, and my long eye-lashes quiver as with sleep. Janusz bends over me, and his gaze seeks to meet mine.

"Look at me!" he whispers, glowing with impatience.

I too am all aglow; yet I turn my head away, and look stubbornly at some cluster of bushes at a distance. But all the time my heart is beseeching him, and saying over and over: "Kiss me, kiss me—now—now—now!"

A moment before, a dress was still looming in the dark in front of us; now we are quite alone. Our eyes have begun to make out the shapes of things; we can discern the trees, and the long narrow strip of pathway where we are walking between two hedges of quickset. Black cloudlike shadows seem now to flee away, now to gather and close upon us.

Suddenly a spasm of horrible unearthly dread clutches at my heart.

"Good God! Look there!" I cry.

"What—what of it?"

I raise my hand to my eyes, and shudder all over with fear, and press close to him.

"There—just beneath us, far, horribly far down—there is water!"

"Well, what of that? There is nothing to be frightened at. I know the garden; it is only a brook which feeds the pond."

"Let us go away—away at once. I saw it glitter through the leaves in the dark: it was so strange! And so deep down: an abyss where I never dreamed the ground sloped at all."

"But we could not fall in: there is a stone barrier."

"No matter," I whisper, half-frantic with dread. "Let us go!"

We make the best of our way back. Janusz is silent, but I feel, as I am holding to his arm, that he too is trembling. He might have quieted me with the words: "Fear nothing by my side!" For but a minute ago, I had boundless confidence in him. Now I know that he can be frightened.

We hear the sounds of the harp and the violin, and a row of lit windows shines on the pitch-black trees.

Janusz breaks the silence. "I have no fear in a forest at night; I fear neither robbers nor wild beasts: but things one cannot explain are not to my liking."

Yes, I quite understand, and share the same dislike: but somehow I had a fancy that . . .

We dance merrily till morning; my painful impression has quite faded.

As we return, we change places; Martha goes with her grandfather, and I am with Janusz. Daybreak shows us a lovely landscape: hills covered with dark woods, fields white with stubble. The sky grows rosy, and we catch ever new glimpses of dim heights, of solitary pear-trees scattered in the fields, of tall sombre poplars in rows, marking the highways in the plain.

We travel long by a road full of deep holes; we climb the heights, we go down into the valleys. All the country round is enchantingly beautiful.

Up comes the sun, casting upon the road distinct mobile shadows, lengthened out monstrously, of our two equipages and of our own figures.

I feel stupefied after this sleepless night; my face is hot, my lips are burning. Yet, and in spite of my plaid and the rugs, I shiver with cold, I close my eyes and lean my head against the back of the carriage, listening to the screaking wheels, to the trot of the snorting horses, and to the timid chirruping of the birds, just roused by daylight. Though awake, I am dreaming.

Janusz bends over me, and touches my lips with his in a gentle kiss, as if he meant not to wake me.

I do not move at all, and pretend to sleep on, though well aware that Janusz knows I am awake.

And now my golden morning—here it is!

On one of the last warm summer days, Martha and I go and bathe together outside the park. When undressed, she is very pleasant to look upon. She pretends to object, but puts on her bathing-dress so deliberately that I can gaze quite at my ease. After having bathed in the clear cool water, we return and lie down on the lush grass in the park. We are surrounded by tall trunks, bare to a great height; far above us their branches form a canopy of bright green verdure under the blue sky.

"I wonder," say I to her, "how plain people feel about themselves. With us, comeliness is such a matter of course! . . . If I were to lose my good looks, or even my knowledge that I am good-looking, I really think I could not bear life. . . . It is that alone which gives me strength in presence of others. I go out in the full glare of day without a sunshade; in company, I sit with my face turned straight to the lamplight; I walk in the crowd, with head erect, fearing no one, abashed by no one—simply because I know that the sight of me must cause pleasure. . . . If I am good-natured, it is because of my good looks. I hate nobody, envy nobody, and am filled with a sort of Pagan, sunshiny, royal love for all."

"And which of us two do you think is prettier?" asks Martha.

"I don't know. . . . In reality, each of us thinks herself prettier; but we are both too cultured ever to have tried conclusions on that subject."

Strictly speaking, I am not so fair as she: but then, she is less graceful than I. Besides, my eyes have a golden tint, such as no other girls have, so far as I know.

I often walk a few versts with Martha, as far as the "Kirkut," or Jewish cemetery.

There they stand, the hewn gravestones, in long parallel upright rows. Upon them you may see cabalistic signs and symbols; a lion, a broken taper, or a shelf of books; and certain embellishments that might almost be styled "decadent." The graves, overgrown with moss, heather, and wild thyme, are nearly level with the rest of the ground. The wooden inclosure, over which we always have to climb, is lost in the woods among the pine-trunks; and those long regular rows of stones raise their heads in a forest elsewhere untouched by man. Here, I feel as though I had gone far back into the dim immemorial Past.

I love that burial-ground; I love to contemplate Life trampling upon Death; and as I gaze, I cease to fear Death any more. Death makes away with the individual only, with the accidental manifestations of Life: Life itself remains. I see myself standing for the whole of mankind, and identical with Life. I always was; I shall be everlasting. . . . Death is slumbering quietly beneath my feet.

And with that a delightful sense, as it were of infinite might, comes over me. To my power, to my continuance, I can find no limit: I am not of the earth, I am not Janka Dernowicz; I am eternal, unsleeping consciousness; I am the Universe! In this burial-ground, Janusz grows dismal, and holds forth on the evanescence of all earthly things. A beautiful animal which lives in fear of Death!

What if it be true that animals have no souls?

At times I experience the pangs of an entirely unjustified longing for the man who came into my life and went out of it like a hurricane. Yes, now and again I long for my ice-plains and my Northern Lights!

Once he asked me whether I should never wish to feel and think and strive along with some companion in life.

Then I burst into laughter; for I hate sentiment—hate to mix up love and "brotherhood of souls."

Now I am near thinking that this man, whom I never loved, may be the only one fit to become my husband.

Often of nights, lying awake and staring into the darkness with wide-open eyes, I feel burning lips, lips famished with hunger, that are pressed to mine. . . .

And when I seize the kiss upon those lips, I know that they are the lips, not of Roslawski, but of Janusz.

And then I am full of terror lest an evil thing has been done that never can be undone —lest something may have fallen away for ever out of my life.

Then do I no longer feel any desire for any one; and I weep in the dark, but silently, not to awaken Martha.

In the morning, I look upon Janusz with hatred and with loathing; and I treat him harshly, though he is indeed in no wise to blame. I merely use him ill, because my soul is a-wandering alone over those ice-plains of mine, is still dreaming cold silvery dreams, is seeking in vain for a fraternal soul.

Is it then really an impossibility to be in love *without loving also?*

While out shooting to-day, Janusz had just such a gleam in his eyes as he has when he gloats on me.

He is a typical primitive man of a nomad race of hunters, in whom the instinct of conservation manifests itself as vehemently when procuring his own subsistence as when acting for the preservation of the race. Game is to him a vital necessity; so is woman.

I was sorry for the hares he had killed and lectured him with great unction on man's cruelty in taking the lives of such defenceless innocent creatures.

Just now I was thinking how I should like to lock Janusz up in a nice cage, and have him all to myself. I should give him plenty of food, but neither let him read (that prohibition he would not find very hard) nor talk to any one; so that he, with all his treasures of vitality, might be mine alone. And occasionally I should enter the cage.

I should then be far more spiritually disposed than I am now. At present, my splendid, primitive, untamed beast is hungry and

howling, and mars the divine symphony I
listen to in my dreams of light.

I should appease it, and go out to walk in
my sacred grove, along the margin of the
dark abysmal lake which is in my soul.

And I should willingly have Roslawski to
walk with me there!

Janusz has asked me if I would consent
to become his wife.

"If only for a month or two, I would with
pleasure," was my truthful reply, which I
afterwards turned into a jest: not a nice one,
I must say.

Janusz darted one or two angry looks at me,
and gave vent to this aphorism: "There are
things one should never jest about."

Most certainly he is right. And all this
begins to worry me just a little.

I might perhaps fancy myself playing the
part of his seductress; of his wife, never.
And what to do with him now, I can't tell.

I should like to go away now. Oh, why
has all this come about so suddenly?

Out boating late in the evening, on the
great pond beyond the park.

I have consented to come here, for I am so wretched, I want to die. And I know that Janusz, whom I have been tormenting all day long, can no longer control himself.

His nerves are racked to the very utmost; it is my doing. He clutches me by the shoulders and holds me down to the side of the boat with an iron grip. To get the better of his mad fit, I keep myself very passive and cool.

"Hear me, Janka!" he growls between his teeth, his face close to mine, "you! listen: I am speaking for the last time. Say Yes!"

I could disarm him with a single cry of pain or fear: but I remain mute. I must have strong sensations to-night.

"I'll kill—I'll kill you! Do you hear? I hate you as much as I love you, and more. Speak instantly—speak!"

His rage is suffocating him; the words stick in his throat. His knee is pressed hard upon my bosom; his nails dig deep into my flesh. With all my strength I stifle a groan, and wait. The boat is careening over more and more, and begins to be water-logged.

"I shall drown you! See, the boat is about to go down! Say Yes!"

Quietly, silently, I look into his wild burning eyes, of which the whites gleam through the darkness and fascinate me.

For an instant I have a desire to close my eyelids and disappear, sinking noiselessly into the dark water. My eyes nevertheless instinctively encounter his.

Suddenly I feel that the grip of his clenched hands is growing weaker.

Now sure of victory, I whisper, "No!" with a smile.

Janusz, uttering a cry of pain, falls back into the boat. He presses his forehead hard against my feet which he covers with kisses, and is swept by a storm of convulsive sobs. The boat recovers her balance, and rocks up and down violently.

But I am the reverse of elated by my victory. For now I can no longer believe in the omnipotence of mere physical strength, which has just shown itself less mighty than the power of Mind.

Had Janusz continued to grapple with me thus for a few seconds more, I think I might have given way to him. And now I envy him the incomparable joy of acknowledging my predominance.

The warrior does not delight in triumphing

over one less strong, but in confessing the power of him that has been found stronger, and by whom he has been overcome.

Over this writhing figure, shaken with sobs that grow fainter and fainter with fatigue, I look out far into the night. No moon, not a star. And the rushes along the shore keep up an incessant rustling.

And the dark lake, my soul, is looking up with unseeing eyes to the dark sky.

All around is dead: no life anywhere. Nothing remains but my loneliness—the unbounded loneliness of my strength, self-centred and unparalleled.

Never yet have I felt my power so strongly, and never yet has it made me so sad.

The black sky bends its lowering vault above me; under its clouds the black pond lifts up swelling waves. Between the Infinite and my soul, there is nowhere any room for strength.

Oh, *"I am so weary, weary of these heights!"* How I desire to meet with a force able to subdue mine!

"Pray, Janusz, pray get up," I say, gently stroking his hair; "I beg you, rise; it must be very late. Where are the oars?"

I am lying in the hollow between two rows of graves, breathing the perfume of the white forest gilliflowers, abloom in the "Kirkut," and thinking of life—of this most admirable and most beautiful marvel, life. I am explaining to Martha how my worship of life is really the outcome of resignation.

"But in me resignation has taken a form that it has not in you. 'If I cannot have all, I refuse to have anything;' such is the creed of despairing pride, held by slaves and wretched men. My belief in Azoism is nothing but the creed of a proud woman, who is reconciled to her slavery, and will take up no spurious imitations of freedom. Such a withdrawal from the vortex we live in, enabling me to look on all things as Garborg does, from above them, and with a smile of dignified amenity—this is what I love. It often seems to me, so little I feel adapted for my life on earth, that I have somehow wandered hither by a mischance, a blunder."

"It is well," says Martha. "Adaptation to environment is of avail only to brute animals: man can make his own world by viewing it in his own special way.

"I," she goes on to say sadly, "believe in

nothing. And yet women in general are inclined to have faith in an existence after death. It is simply an outcome of sympathy with suffering, and of an instinct of justice. You know how the thought of useless suffering in nature makes me beside myself. Think of all those silent agonies which never will be known; of those tortures endured throughout the world by multitudes that leave no trace behind them. . . . When but a little boy, Janusz once focussed the sun's rays on a little insect he had fastened by its wing, and which was writhing in impotent throes. I can still see those poor limbs, red in the glow, quivering in excruciating pain, until I snatched the lens away from Janusz, and set the half-roasted creature free. . . . Those were its last impressions of life: after them came —Nothingness! I can see all the tiny invisible beings that I slay by hundreds in my daily walks, trampling them down in the long grass or under the pine-needles, and unwittingly leaving them to expire in the most dreadful torments, perhaps drawn out for many an hour. . . . I know, too, of the pain which fishes undergo, often kept living in the air for whole days, and seen to move convulsively, even when on the fire. . . . All this pain, and nothing to justify, nothing to compensate it! This I know; for beyond death there is nothing!"

"But did it never strike you that, if there is nothing beyond death, it is impossible for *nothingness* to be there?"

She looks at me inquiringly.

"The ideas of justice, of vengeance, of compensation, are purely of this earth, though they once formed a religious ideal in the worship of Jehovah. I put them in the same category as the concept of mercy, now prevailing amongst Christians. Some other idea will spring up later, equally foreign to that of existence beyond the grave."

"Well, and what do you infer from that?"

"My belief is, that the phenomenon called death consists in our losing all sensations, 'categories,' concepts and all projections (so to speak) of this our world; and in our finding *other* sensations in the next. Perhaps not even that. For in the next world, just as there will be no idea of justice, so there may be none of sensations. Do you follow me?"

"So you think you shall continue to exist then?"

"I cannot say—I cannot say."

For a few minutes I listen to the undertone of the pine-trees, sounding far above us in the sky.

"You see," I continue, "there, it may well be, we shall have no idea of an Ego which excludes and contradicts the Non-Ego. The distinction between them has arisen from the fact of our existence upon earth: it is a form into which we mould our impressions; something purely accidental, depending upon the quality and mechanism of the brain. . . . There, too, the idea of Time may be wanting; also that of Space. Of course, from our earthly point of view, it is nonsense to say that the world is boundless: that which the brain calls 'the Infinite' cannot be represented in imagination as space. Truly, there are times when I simply feel admiration for a God who has created so great and endlessly complicated a scheme of beings."

Martha's disappointment is plain to perceive.

"So then you believe in God?"

"I do not know, and do not trouble about it. It is not likely the ideas of creation out of nothing, of sovereignty as opposed to subjection, of volition as opposed to passiveness, have any counterpart out of our minds. . . . Notice, Martha, that in my view the expression, 'Transcendental Being,' implies a contradiction. Our very idea of Being is a mere outcome of experience: and I go so far beyond Nature, I leap so completely out of my human skin, that I can force myself to the contemplation of an unimaginable world, in which there is no contradiction between Being and Non-Being. . . .

"Therefore, I do not trouble whether I shall in that world be myself or not myself: nor even whether I shall be or not be. . . ."

She gazes at me, her eyes wide open, and says under her breath:

"Yes, I see."

"And, do you know, the capacity of thus abstracting one's thought itself from its outward form, of looking upon the universe and one's very thought from such a standpoint, sets one on heights incomprehensibly sublime, and gives the purest, the most unearthly delight."

. . . There is a black cat here, with eyes like emeralds; it ranges noiselessly amongst the rows of gravestones. A singu-

larly sociable creature; it follows us everywhere in our walks, like a dog. . . . When
I look at it, I cannot help believing in
Metempsychosis: there must dwell within
this cat some very refined aristocratic soul, one
that looks upon everything with supreme
scepticism.

"What is the matter, Martha?"

"Nothing. I have only dropped a hairpin."

A tortoise-shell pin has fallen out of her
thick black tresses, and dropped on to the
earth with a faint sound.

Martha is just now in a very lofty mood.
This real world of ours strikes her as a contrast, ridiculous in its littleness, to the world
we are speaking of. So she does not wish
me to pick up that pin, though it has dropped
quite close to me on the heather. To my
mind this is too high-flown, too girlish.
After all, the realities of life are paramount,
and we ought to have so much intellectual culture as never to forget it.

Wherefore I give her the pin, smiling very
sarcastically.

"After all," I conclude, rising from the
hollow ridge and preparing to walk home,
"I quite understand that what I have said

amounts to the same as belief in nothing. It is all the same to me whether I shall cease to be after death, or be transferred to a world wherein there is no idea of being, or of any Ego, conditioning my self-consciousness. I understand, too, that a world in which Being does not contradict Non-Being, is to our minds equivalent to no world at all. So that my faith is similar to your unfaith, but inferred and formulated otherwise."

Janusz is very humble and wretched now. Sometimes, when we sit long together of an evening, he will fall asleep with his head in my lap, worn out with nervous exhaustion. And then I am face to face with something very strange.

I feel a mysterious dread of the torment of an everlasting vigil, together with a sense of responsibility beyond my strength. Yet I do not wake him, although I am shuddering with dread; I will not let him know that I am afraid! . . . There are certain things one should not speak about to children. . . . That I love solitude when alone, but that the feeling of solitude when some one is by me, fills me with unspeakable dread, for then I

hear my soul uttering her triumphant laugh:
this I would never confess to him.

Vigorous I am, and able to struggle for a
long time. But even for warriors there come
moments when they trustfully lay their tired
heads on some one's lap; when they feel se-
cure in the knowledge of some one above
them, watching over them, standing between
them and their foes, between them and the
Infinite, the Unknown.

Is there any man in the world who could
thus lull my watchfulness to sleep? There is
one, only one. But the price I should pay
would be all that makes life charming.

When Janusz is sleeping on my lap, I then
invariably think of—Roslawski.

As a rule, it is from a novelist's or an artist's standpoint—from without and objectively—that I view whatever happens in my
life; consciously throwing all my impressions
into the form of sentences, rounded and complete, often affected and unnatural; and in
everything I say, think, or do, seeking for
dramatic, literary, or picturesque effects.
This peculiarity I hold for one of the tragic

sides of my life, since it almost entirely robs my impressions of their directness.

People sometimes blame me for being mannered, for attitudinizing, for performing everything with artifice, whether I make a bow or do my hair. And I fully admit they are right. But then, artificiality comes naturally to me. Every motion, every smile of mine is present to me before it is elicited: it is scrutinized and judged by me, as though I were some one else. For me, there is no present; I look at all things from out of the Future: there are no involuntary bursts of thought, no inarticulate words or mechanical gestures for me. And should I try to behave with apparent artlessness, I should then be artificial twice over.

This afternoon a carriage, covered with mud, and drawn by a couple of splendid sorrel horses, pulls up in front of our terrace. Imszanski jumps out, throwing the reins to the groom, who sits behind. Janusz welcomes him, and he slowly comes up the steps. He has driven thirty-five miles, but his impassive features bear not the slightest trace of fatigue.

He improves upon acquaintance. Beyond all doubt, he is the handsomest man I know: a great point in his favour. His movements, characterized by a certain graceful languor, betray his noble descent; in his bright eyes there is to be seen continual concentrated thought and tranquil, half-forgotten sorrow. He has every accomplishment, talks interestingly, elegantly, with literary turns and expressions; he has at his call every variety of smile but never laughs outright. Considerate restraint is his speciality.

His first words on entering are: "My sister sends you her greetings: she wanted to come with me, but I was afraid to take her. It is so long a journey, and the roads are in so bad a state now."

He pays court both to Martha and to myself with equal politeness; with her he is more serious, with me more gallant. Which is the proper thing, as I am a visitor in the neighbourhood.

I am all but enchanted, and my eyes are continually fixed on him. And yet at the same time I know that this paragon of a man could never succeed in winning my love. From a physical point of view, I care even less for him than for Roslawski. This, I suppose, is precisely on account of his marvellous beauty, which may draw off my attention from him as a man and an intelligent being. I could gaze with just as much enthusiasm on his portrait.

We go out to inspect some new kinds of ornamental shrubs which Martha has recently had planted in the park. Janusz walks with me; Imszanski with Martha, a few paces before us.

These two make a pretty picture, on which I like to gaze. In this grand old park, they remind me of the days of yore, and the knights and their lady-loves. Martha, I remark, has a style and breeding that I lack. To help her over a plash of water, Imszanski gives her his hand. She gathers up her dress, just revealing her neat and shapely ankles. The pair are just like dancers in a minuet, and so handsome that I cannot find it in my heart to envy them.

Janusz walks at my side like a shadow, and follows my glances with eyes ablaze.

"A fine man, Imszanski: you like him, don't you?" he asks. "But," he goes on to say, "I don't advise you to try your hand on him: he is another's. Has loved long and hopelessly."

"Has he?"

"When in Warsaw, he went the length of attempting suicide—unsuccessfully, I need not say."

"But this love of his, is it not only hopeless, but unrequited too?"

"Well, he proposed—and was refused. But that's no wonder. Such a man should never marry; a whole seraglio would not be enough for him."

"H'm, yes; that would be quite in his line. Who is the girl? Does she live near?"

"Yes, she does."

"And who may she be? Please tell me. Was she at the Sedniewski party?"

"Don't ask; I must not tell. It has been kept secret."

"But did anybody confide in you?"

"Why, no."

"Then I have as much right to know as you have. I am awfully curious, and wonder at the girl's taste. . . . Do I know her?"

He holds out for some time, but in the end I disarm him: though in the way I dislike most and very seldom employ, . . . by wheedling and coaxing him. The secret shall go down to the grave with me, I promise him. He hesitates awhile; then says in an undertone:

"Martha."

I do my best to conceai my unbounded astonishment under some commonplace expressions of faint surprise. I obviously have not the slightest intention to keep my word: I will ask Martha about the whole business. Can she possibly not be in love with such a Phœnix? Can she too have found him undesirable because of that beauty of his?

During supper I watch her closely, and see in her face that very same pallor, that very look of weariness and constraint that she was wearing in Topolow. No, his love is certainly not unrequited.

I have no fondness, and consequently no fellow-feeling, for the girl: but now I am more interested than before in her theory of "Azoism." I formerly thought she had taken it up as an apology for her life; now I see that her life itself compels her to profess it.

Imszanski himself is always the same, courteous and languidly good-humoured.

He is talking with Martha's grandfather
about this year's crops, and looking quite interested in the subject.

It is a cool windy autumn day. Clouds are
floating close to the earth, rain is in the air,
and no birds are seen. Along the woods
stretch the fields, either already harrowed, or
covered with dingy whitish stubble. Something has gone out of my life forever: I cannot get rid of the thought.

We three are riding together over the desolate plain. Janusz rides in front of us, playing acrobatic tricks on horseback, and really
performing wonderful feats of agility.

But it is now ebb-tide with me. Those
tight trousers, those raw leather boots of his
—I hate them, and scorn myself for having
let that sort of thing ever make any impression on me; assuredly there is nothing in all
this that is worthy of scorn.

Autumn has come. That is all.

We come abreast upon the muddy high-
way, all three strangely sick at heart. In silence we ride on.

Latterly Janusz has altered very much.
His face is pale; it is the face of a man lost

in troubled thought. When we are by ourselves, he scarcely ever raises his eyes to
mine; and his outbursts of energy resemble
the frenzy of delirium. After the equestrian
evolutions just performed, he looks wearied
and gloomy, and his lips are closed fast as he
rides.

Why is each of us thus? I alone can tell.
Because Martha is thinking of Imszanski, and
Janusz of me, and I am thinking of Roslawski. It is just like a novel: each of us as remote as one star is from another.

I got a post-card from Obojanski yesterday, saying he had come back; so I shall have
to be off in four days. I must then see Roslawski, who has no doubt returned to Warsaw
by now. A fever of impatience possesses me.

On my return, I lie down on the drawing-
room sofa, still in my riding-habit.

Martha, as usual, is journeying from pan-
try to cellar, Janusz has gone to dress for supper; "Grandfather" is probably asleep in
some nook. I feel maddened with impatience
at the thought of seeing Him again. I tear
my hair, sobbing noiselessly and without
tears.

My misery is at its height. And now, be-

sides, I feel this: that I am sorry to go away
—sorry for Janusz. Something there is
within me, tearing at my soul—tearing it to
bits, to shreds, to tatters.

I hear Janusz coming, take up an easy re-
cumbent attitude, without rising from the
sofa, and arrange my hair.

"What! you here already?" I remark in a
peevishly flippant tone of inquiry.

He does not reply, but draws near with
noiseless reverent steps, in an attitude of supreme worship, such as an idolator may pay
to the idol he distractedly adores. Kneeling
down before me, he gently takes my hands and
presses them to his brow. I do not withdraw them. I lean forwards instinctively.

"Janka, listen," he says tenderly, in a voice
that trembles with suppressed emotion; "say
that you will be my wife; say so, my dear.
. . . You know what you have made of
me. . . . You laughed at me for my so-
ber-mindedness, my shallow outlook upon
life, my thoughtless *joie de vivre*. Now I am
quite different. . . . Now I am like you,
and like the rest of your set. . . . Could
I ever, in the old days, have thought it possible that I should become like a child—cry-

ing my eyes out at the thought of your going away, Janka? I have nothing in the world to console me but you . . . Janka, since you told me you were sorry for the hares I had killed, I have not gone out shooting any more. . . . Oh, I shall not struggle with you, I should not get the mastery; but as your slave, I beg you, I entreat you, be my wife! Oh, my adorable lady, my most sweet one, say but that you will! You will be happy; you will see me do everything, everything to please you. . . . You will live like a princess. . . . If you will not give me this assurance, I shall go to ruin, indeed I shall. Janka, I will leave the University without taking my degree. . . . I will follow you everywhere on earth. Martha, too; does she not love you? And does it matter to you if you say Yes now? Nothing hinders you from saying the word; I even think you love me just a little. . . . Oh, Janka, Janka!"

He ends with a burst of tears. My head bends down to his, and we both weep together. In turns I am rent by compassion for him and by my longing for Roslawski. I kiss his black silky curls, and we cry like children.

Finally we agree that I shall go to Warsaw "to take counsel with my family and with my own heart"; and I am to give him a definite answer in a month's time.

By then I shall surely have seen Roslawski —and everything will have been settled: for life or for death.

Every morning, the trees in the park are now white with hoarfrost, and we find the threshing-floor in the barn covered with many a steel-blue swallow, lying frozen to death. The stoves are heated, the windows hermetically closed (for the time being), and, though autumn has but just commenced, we are in winter quarters already.

In the calm white country house, sleep reigns supreme.

The wild wind howls through the sombre shrubberies, and sweeps showers of drifting leaves, green but frost-bitten, along the walls of the park. Through the windows I look out into the cold bleak night, a night of desolation and evil omen: such a night as one might expect to bring us mysterious half-frozen travellers who have lost their way; and on this very night they should come knocking at the door. The old, faithful, superstitious servants should mutter the saying: "Some one has hanged himself, the wind is so high," and the dogs should howl together mournfully.

There is no light save in one window, by which, through the broad chinks in the shutters, its bright streaks filter out into the park. The maids are there, keeping vigil as usual; Janusz and the old man have gone to bed and have long been asleep.

Around there breathes that stillness and quiet sense of security which a winter night is wont to bring with it—an atmosphere of repose.

I am kneeling by the fire, in a plain dressing-gown, with my hands clasped behind my head, and my eyes fixed upon the flames. Flashes of red light up my dark face and my chestnut hair. Now and then I put big logs on the fire from the heap close at hand; I like to resemble a vestal virgin.

Martha, partly undressed and without her corset, lies dejectedly smoking a cigarette on a rose-coloured couch, not looking in my direction.

She absent-mindedly strokes a cat, which

lies close to her and purrs loudly, pretending to be pleased but cross in fact, because she wants to sleep, and Martha prevents her.

"I shall be so bored when you leave us, Janka," she says. "There will be a sad void all over the place."

"Then come with me to Warsaw."

"Somebody must remain to keep house at Klosow; besides, Grandfather cannot be left alone. I shall not be free till after a year's time, when Janusz has finished his course of agronomy."

"Do you know, Martha, you remind me of a heroine in an old-fashioned novel and I don't care for variety. You are too goody-goody. Such a pity as it is to waste a year of one's youth. . . . You may quite well leave everything to the steward's care. . . . Remember, you will soon be twenty-five, and life never goes back."

"But I am glad—how glad!—that it does not."

"That's a pose, or a mere high-flown mood. You love life in spite of all."

Turning towards her, I meet her earnest gaze—calm, and yet, oh! how mournful!

"I hate life, Janka!" she replies.

Silence follows. The cat leaps from off the couch, stretches herself, and makes for the fireplace with leisurely velvet tread. She rubs herself against me, lies down in the full glare of the hearth, and instantly falls asleep.

"Once," Martha continues, "I saw them kill a black sheep, as I had told them to do. A clean-shaven old farm-labourer first tied its legs, and then sharpened his knife on a whetstone for a long time. Finally, he turned its beautiful tapering head on one side, and deliberately, skilfully, drew the knife backwards and forwards across its throat. And the poor animal did not so much as shrink: never did it once bleat, or show the least sign of reluctance. I wanted to run away, or cover my eyes, or at least turn from the sight: but I forced myself to undergo that internal agony, in order to atone for the quiet death of that meek, harmless beast. I asked the labourer afterwards whether he was not sorry for killing it. He answered me: 'Why should I be? It was my lady's order. I would cut a man's throat for her, if she told me to.'

"Once my threshing-machine killed a man. Corn had been stolen, and I had to watch the men by myself, the steward being away at the time. They had stolen it, because I had more than they. . . . I remember the man leaning forwards incautiously—a horrible cry—a dull grinding sound—and a sudden silence. The machine had stopped; out of it they took only a bleeding mass. I made the dead man's widow a life-pension, and saw to the bringing-up of the children. And because of that, they call me benefactress and angel!

"Or again. A woman of seventeen died in child-bed. Three days and three nights she lay howling in the farm-servants' quarters, howling like a wounded beast, so that I could hear her even in my own room. Well, she died at last; but the boy survived. He is now three years old, he laughs in the sunshine, cuts earthworms to pieces for a pastime, and tears off cockchafers' legs.

"Kosa, a peasant here, had a son who was dying slowly of consumption. The priest was sent for, and brought him the last sacraments. Outside the hut, he had to bargain with Kosa about the burial fees.

"Once, in our pond, the loathsome swollen corpse of a new-born child came floating to the surface. What harm had it ever done? Possibly it was put to death because its life of a day or two had made it the instrument of some wrong done!

"Janka, I hate life!"

"Listen," I say, casting my eyes down. "I —I don't know how to begin; that is, I wanted to tell you that it may be I am leaving you only for a short time. In a few weeks, I shall perhaps be here again."

"I wish you would," she replies. "Janusz is in a pitiful state."

Another pause ensues. I am thinking how far indeed I am from such a wish; and I feel something rising in my throat. Suddenly I decide to speak now.

"Martha," I say, "tell me the reason why you refused Imszanski." She starts, and stares at me with eyes like a frightened deer's.

"Fear nothing," I say, reassuringly. "You must not think I shall inflict compassion on you; I am only calmly and objectively interested. Tell me: can you possibly not be in love with so amazingly handsome a man?"

She is silent a while, debating with herself; and then:

"Yes, I was in love with him," she replies, in a calm low voice.

"Well, and have you sacrificed your happiness to that abstract theory of yours?"

Another pause.

"Not exactly. . . . The fact is that I simply could not bear to think I had not been his only love."

There she stops, but I feel she is only waiting for me to question her further: this is the moment when she must lay bare to me what she has hitherto, with her wonted secretiveness, concealed from every eye. Yet I refrain from questions.

Again she speaks, slowly and as one that looks back on memories that are still fresh: "We often spent the winter evenings together. His soul was the thing nearest and dearest to me on earth, but I loved him yet more because his eyes were so mournful and his lips so fine.

"He may have been too outspoken: he desired I should know all about him, before I plighted my troth. I wish I had known nothing; there is bliss only where there is ignorance. . . . For there have been some instants of forgetfulness; and these have given me an inkling of what my happiness would

have been—how immense, how incredible—
had I been his only love in the past, as I am
(it yet may be) his only love in the present.

"It was on a most beautiful winter's night,
silvery in the moonbeams, that I saw it pass
before me, that long procession of women, fair
as the flowers of spring: 'a connoisseur in
women' is what they call him. A whole garden of red flowers sprang up in the snowy
wilderness, shining afar like a great pool of
gore. I closed my eyes with the torture of
the sight.

"If it be true that love consists of happiness
and delight, then all this delight ought to have
been mine: and Life had taken it from me:
not to give it to others, but just to throw it
away (ah! the crime of it!) to fritter it away
amongst a multitude of delights *that might
have been.* For indeed, what would have
made my bliss was a wrong inflicted upon
others, in the form of compulsion and shame,
the torment of humiliation, the infringement
of their right to live, hurling them into an
abyss of misery and abandonment, and closing the gates against their return to a happier state:—all these deeds of wrong-doing
were acts that might have given me bliss! . . .

"Now, it came that in one of those moments of oblivion, when I felt I was happy, I told him I would be his affianced wife.

"Then he gathered me in his arms—Oh, with what a movement, admirable in its tenderness—and pressed me gently to his heart, that he might kiss my lips.

"And then came the most astonishing instant in all my life. I had, to put it simply, a vision. Upon his lips I saw blood—clotted, dried blood—the ashes as it were of thousands and thousands of kisses. It was neither loathing nor hatred that I felt; only an exceeding horror for what is as much against Nature as was any elaborate excruciating torture of Mediæval times—as a crime committed in secret and hidden under flowers to conceal its every trace. And from beneath those flowers —a sea of them there was—I seemed to hear the groans as it were of those slain at some banquet of Heliogabalus: or rather I heard laughter, artificial, forced, metallic laughter— the laughter which 'women of that sort' always utter, it being the paid merriment to which they are bound:—such a laugh as breaks off suddenly, abruptly, as though startled at its own sound. And I saw my white lilies plunged in that sea of tainted blood!

"So I repulsed him, as I would have repulsed a foe. And here," she concluded suddenly, in a falsetto of spasmodic laughter, "here my little idyll comes to an end."

"But do you love the man still?"

"I do."

From the farmyard comes the crowing of a cock: as a key that grates in a rusty lock, it grates on our ears. Dawn is here.

I like the man; or it may be that I rather like his surroundings, inseparably connected in thought with him. I like those rooms of severe aspect, with their high ceilings, and shelves which are nearly as high filled with books, all in regular order and bound in black. I like the great table in the centre, lit up with bright lamps, and strewn with periodicals in every language. I like, too, those heavy, comfortable, leather-covered arm-chairs which stand round it. Obojanski also I like, who in this environment is a handsome man, with grey hair and eyes dark and youthful.

Formerly my professor, Obojanski has been extremely useful to me in my studies. The profit I have derived from him is, however, chiefly negative, from the critical side of his teaching. It still pleases him, in our mutual relations, to take up the attitude of a master.

Generally I come to him late in the evening, dressed in black, in the style of "la dame voilée." If he is working, I sit with him, and set to reading some interesting book: but we mostly converse together, and invariably of serious things.

Obojanski is an old bachelor, and objects to women as a rule. "The idea of emancipation, possibly not quite unreasonable in principle, has been misunderstood and warped from its true meaning by the women themselves. For instance, they are not content with equality in the field of economics; they want to have the same freedom in their conduct as is enjoyed by men. A fine place the world would be, if they had! And, as concerns the admission of women to the higher studies, this is absolutely superfluous: a woman's brain is not able to think with the logical accuracy which these require."

"As to this last," I reply, "a census of the sexes would not, I think, be desirable. It may well be doubted, not only whether all males, but whether all learned men, are capable of accurate logical reasoning."

"Oh, of course, exceptions are everywhere to be found," he answers gravely, with his own peculiar directness of mental association.

To his mind, I am among women one of those exceptions. He is never scandalized at my late visits; perhaps only for the reason that my visits are made to him. He is withal full of respect for my intellectual capacity, which he thinks due to him. For him, I am the one woman who can talk reasonably.

For my own part, I do not consider myself to be clever merely for being able to draw a logical conclusion from two premises. What I call cleverness is the faculty of understanding all things, and of wondering at none; that of setting aside all preconceived ideas and doctrines, by reason of which men have set up "categories," and of giving up accepted forms of thinking, that seem to be, but are not, necessary to thought; the faculty of getting out of oneself, and viewing both oneself and everything else from without and objectively.

I sit down in one of the high-backed armchairs, and begin to talk about some abstruse subject or other, but making every endeavour to lead the conversation round to Roslawski.

"Do you know London?" I ask.

"Oh, yes; I was there; a long time ago, when I had just finished my University studies."

"I think Roslawski went there for about six months."

"Yes, and he is there still."

My strength has just been put to the test, and I am satisfied. The news I hear neither makes my lips tremble, nor dims my dark-golden eyes with the slightest mist. But I am careful not to pretend either indifference or special good humour. Obojanski, in spite of his weak points, is no mean expert in the knowledge of human nature.

"Indeed! Why, I was informed he had returned to Warsaw already."

"No. I am expecting him about the middle of this month. He is a nice fellow, is he not? We three got on very well together."

"I hope you don't mean that we two do not get on well," I answer, smiling amiably.

He shows me a post-card that he has got from Roslawski: water, some shipping, and an ugly building ashore, with innumerable windows. I for the first time see his handwriting: sloping, not very legible; nothing much out of the ordinary. I should like to press it to my lips, which would be a piece of highly unjustifiable sentimentalism.

Greatly as I want to go home, and—like a child—have "a good cry" all by myself, I stay on there for some time. Obojanski offers me several books, dealing mostly with matters zoölogical. I of course try to excuse myself as best I can. At last, he lectures me on the way I am wasting my talents, and says that my mind, "if deprived of intellectual nourishment, will pine away."

"But, Professor," I point out, not without a touch of pride, "I really am not at all naturally fitted to be a woman of scientific attainments."

"Ah, but have a little faith in yourself; you ought to. Truly, science is your exclusive vocation; but you must work; you need to work a good deal. With your abilities . . ."

I go home, taking the books with me. My room is dark and dreary and solitary. I am most bitterly disappointed.

I have done a silly thing to-day.
A girl named Nierwiska works in the office

with me. I like her best of all, because she
is the prettiest. Both her looks and her get-
up are in rather consistent Japanese style; a
style that makes her look limp and drooping
under the burden of her own hair. Now, on
my return from the holidays, I had noticed
that she was much changed and extremely
dejected.

To-day, contrary to my custom, I left the
office with her, and it turned out that our way
home was the same for a good distance.

Our conversation runs at first on indifferent matters. Nierwiska answers briefly, in
low tones, now and then casting a somewhat
suspicious glance towards me. Women have
intuition; and she, less cultured than Martha,
is averse to purely objective curiosity. I feel
that, at any question too bluntly put, she will
shut her lips fast, shrink back into herself,
and close up like a mimosa leaf; and this
makes me doubly cautious. Our talk turns
upon the general lot of women who earn their
bread.

"Those who are forced to work for their
livelihood," she says in musical tones, "are
apt to fall into a chronic state of dreariness,
even when no real and tangible cause is there."

"You are right. Certainly, there are people who cannot understand how it is possible to feel sad, so long as no harm is done them. But for us, life itself is an evil; it harms us."

"Because of the work we have to do."

"Then don't you like your work?"

"On the contrary. I should like it, but . . ."

"Well, but what?"

"In general, I can work with a pretty good will; but just now I am so weary and so upset. . . ."

We are now in front of the house where Nierwiska is living. As we take leave of each other, I draw her into the doorway, and ask her in a whisper:

"You are in love, are you not?"

She starts away from me in a flutter of shyness. I stroke her hand soothingly.

"And things don't go smoothly, eh? Tell me."

She hangs her head, and replies, in an earnest childlike tone:

"No, they do not."

"What! does he not love you?"

"Perhaps he does—just a little. But I must tell you, with me, self-respect comes first of

all. . . . I cannot . . . Even should I be
forced to break it all off, I will have nothing
to blush for."

I look at her attentively, not without surprise: till now, I had not known her to be of
this stamp.

"As for me," I suddenly burst out, "as for
me,—if the man who ruined my life, and took
his leave without even a smile or a kind word
of farewell, were only to beckon me to him
to-day, I would at once follow him like a
lamb!"

Then, in the rough, free and easy way of
comrades at work, I bid her good-bye with a
hand-shake, and walk swiftly away from her
door, depressed and uncomfortable; humbled,
in a word.

And now, I am in a most vile humour. She
has shown herself far more clear-headed than
I have. By means of a few commonplaces,
she has forced from me an avowal that I never
would have made, no, not even to Martha
herself! . . . A pose,—in part at least,—that
prodigious self-respect of hers. All the same,
she is sacrificing her love to it.

Strange creatures they are! Take Martha's
case: purity! why, she was raving about it.

Nothing should stand in my way, if I loved; and therefore no doubt I cannot meet with love anywhere.

I often call upon Obojanski now, in the dim semi-conscious hope that I may meet him there. And each of my visits is only a fresh disappointment.

This "hope deferred" is working me up beyond all bearing; and the bitterness of my suffering makes me long for him yet more impatiently and more fondly. Really, I begin to believe that I love the man.

I care no longer for songs, for dances, for flowers. I dream of a strange life, a cold out-of-the-way life,—he and I together,—nay, a life from which kisses should be shut out. I cannot tell why, but I somehow fancy I could not bring myself to kiss that hard, firm-set mouth. Nothing binds me to him—nothing but the sway of his keen, icy glance. And yet, I live in the belief that he is destined to be mine, that no one else shall be my husband.

I went to Obojanski to-day, in order to return to him (unread) a monograph about some species of insect.

From the ante-room I could hear a man's voice.

My heart gave a bound of joy, mingled
with trepidation; it was stilled again at once.

It was, as I presently found out, the voice
of Smilowicz, a former pupil of Obojanski:
an ugly little man, who makes people laugh a
great deal, not by his wit, but by his queer,
comical grimaces.

"I must begin by telling you quite frankly,"
he says, turning to me, "that at first sight I
thought you hateful; you had all the outward
appearance of a fine lady. It was only when
the Professor had explained to me that you
were an accountant and worked for your living, that my hatred changed into sympathy
for you."

His hearty laugh infects me with a gaiety
so artificial that it almost gives me pain.

"Your compliment, paid in so negative a
form, I cannot doubt to be sincere; as such
it is a novelty. But I have not the least wish
to make my appearance symbolize the dreary
lot of a woman who works."

Obojanski, somewhat annoyed, remarks:
"Alas! that even the cleverest of her sex
should have this little bit of vanity!"

I glance at his form, gracefully leaning
back in his easy-chair, clad in a fine suit of

black cloth; at his trousers, beautifully
creased, his nicely-tied cravat, and his silvery
beard in perfect trim; and I smile silently.
I shall not tell him what comes to my mind:
he would directly begin to protest that his
clothing is as unpretentious as can be; neither
dirty nor untidy, but nothing more. Now all
these half-conscious, but innumerable, little
insincerities, are distasteful to me: there is
something unmanly about them.

"Vanity is nothing but the æsthetic feeling
in its maturity. Undoubtedly it contains an
element of coquetry, but the latter has its
source in the reproductive instinct." This I
say, seriously, but speaking quickly, to hide
what I feel; adding, "It is by a woman's
clothing that her individuality and degree of
artistic culture are made known."

"Individuality? In the fetters of fashion?
Bah!"

"Well, what is fashion after all? It only
expresses variations in the preferences of human beings: just like the various periods in
literature and art and history."

Smilowicz interferes. "Yes, but these variations of preference should be free, not en-
forced."

"There is no help for that. In every sphere
of life we meet with individuals who have
happy thoughts, and with crowds who imitate
them. No one orders them to imitate: they
do so willingly, driven by the force of other
people's opinions, because they neither think
nor act for themselves. Besides, is the following of fashion necessarily a spirit of imita-
tion? It is very often, as it were, something
infectious in the air we breathe. Short
sleeves succeed to long ones, sleeves puffed.
about the wrists, to sleeves puffed at the shoulders: just as Idealism comes after Realism,
and as Mysticism reigns where Positivism
reigned once."

"Tut, tut, tut," says the Professor, "there is
some difference between literature and dress."

"Oh, surely . . . Now, every general trend
should allow particular tendencies to come
into play, and it is just in these that individuality is manifested. And that's why I simply cannot bear male attire, with its never-
changing stiffness and lifelessness of form."

"Ah, but do you not see that this fixed.
standard is the 'great leveller of classes,'
which annihilates inequalities in social standing? Attired as I am, there is no difference

between me and a shoemaker in his Sunday suit."

Once again, the insincerity, the cheap semi-conscious coquetry of these words, is disagreeable to me. No one looking at him could help seeing that a shoemaker, were he clad in those very garments, would be otherwise attired than he. And this Obojanski is perfectly well aware of.

"That," I make answer, "is just what is wrong with men's clothing; it excludes the manifestation of what in reality exists, and, by removing the outward show of an evil, it helps us to forget its presence. I do not think that to be at all right."

"Yes," Smilowicz chimes in with his funny smile, "its result for you, Professor, would be that people, taking you for a shoemaker, might fancy you to be an honest man who gets his bread by his work alone."

The notes of Grieg's *Der Frühling* just now recur to my mind: they so strongly recall those evenings I spent with Martha. I was happier then: every present good is always greatly magnified, when past. I now look back on Klosow as on a Paradise—to which I shall never return!

Something grievous is awaiting me here. And, meanwhile, he does not come—he does not come!

"There are times when I doubt whether I am doing well to awake your mind so early, and raise doubts on all the points you were accustomed to believe in. I fear you may find such views an intolerable weight upon your mind, and lose yourself in the maze of my own sceptical musings."

With these words, Obojanski winds up a long lecture that tends to prove there is no such thing as a God, and that the soul is but a function of the body. I smile at his fears, which (I assure him) are quite groundless: I am not in danger of any doubt whatever on things fundamental.

"I now see that I look upon you as a friend, and talk to you about everything. I forget that you are a woman—and as yet all but a little girl."

And here the electric bell rings; its tinkle announces nothing out of the common to me!

"Who has come so late?" I ask, trembling all over.

"Roslawski, very likely. . . . He arrived

yesterday, and wrote that he would be here; but I was not expecting him any longer."

I hear the servant's steps in the ante-room, and the door as it opens. Obojanski leaves the room, and presently I recognize that voice —*his* voice! He is explaining the cause of his delay in coming.

"Have you any one with you?" he asks, evidently averse to seeing strangers now.

"No, no; only Smilowicz and Miss Dernowicz, whom you know. . . . Come along."

This time my self-control has quite forsaken me, and I feel my face on fire. . . . My first impulse is to jump up from my chair and welcome him; fortunately, I have not the strength to rise.

I keep silence, hanging down my head, so as to conceal the working of my features. Smilowicz says something to me, but I cannot make out what.

In comes Roslawski; I bow without looking him in the face; indeed, I scarce raise my head at all.

I am terribly afraid I shall do some unexpected thing. A wild unaccountable terror comes over me, such as one feels when about to faint. I clench my teeth, expectant.

After a while, my nervousness passes away, and I can hear myself asking him about his voyage, about England, about the sea; the calm indifference of my own voice is a surprise to me.

The first coherent thought which strikes me is—that I am a handsome woman: that I *must* be handsome. Roslawski is talking to Obojanski; it is a long time since they met, and they must be left to themselves a little while. I get up from my arm-chair and go towards Smilowicz, who stands silently by, looking at a new book on one of the shelves. Cool, majestic, with head erect and bright eyes shining serenely in the gas-light, I walk by, close to Roslawski. I see myself as from without, clad in a clinging black dress, wearing a great soft and quaintly designed autumn hat; with outlines that form a graceful silhouette, slow movements, picturesque in their indolence, the outcome of a superfluity of latent vital force, kept down and subdued by the will.

For the first time now I cast my eyes upon him, and meet that cold, critical glance of his. No one but myself has ever hitherto been able to look at me in such wise.

I am standing by Smilowicz, and stoop

down with a motion full of elegance and grace, to read the title of the book he is perusing. And all the time I know that the other's cold glance is fixed on me.

"You have changed very considerably during the vacation, Miss Dernowicz," Roslawski says to me, in an undertone audible in the quiet room.

"Have I?" This I say with a smile, raising my head.

"Yes, you seem taller now, and more like a 'grown-up.' Last year there was still something of the schoolgirl in your appearance."

I protest, laughingly, and try to talk with Smilowicz. But instead of listening to him, I am thinking.

Roslawski is to my mind not so much a man as a mechanical power, something of a nature that is hostile and full of hatred; something dangerous; a mesmeric influence. This tall, well-dressed, well-informed gentleman in glasses is not to my mind a living man: rather a sort of abstract idea. At times I can scarce believe him to have any personal existence at all.

I have somehow the impression that I am standing upon a railway track, in a whirlwind

of frozen snow.   Above the howling of the
blast, I hear the thunder of an approaching
train; but I remain rooted to the spot, my
eyes fixed upon the cold unfeeling glare from
the lamps of the engine rushing on and going
to crush me:—rooted there as in a dreadful
nightmare, and unable to take my eyes away
from those calm and ever-dazzling lights.
There I stand, waiting, powerless, full of hostility yet of self-abasement.

Tea is brought, and the conversation becomes general.   To the atmosphere that always reigns at Obojanski's, Roslawski now
brings a newly imported stock of British ici-
ness and rigidity.   We all are sensible of the
bonds of I know not what invisible etiquette,
enveloping and wrapping us up like subtle,
unbreakable cobwebs: we no longer venture
to laugh out loud; everything is suppressed
and stiff and grey.

"So then," he says, without for a second
taking his eyes off me during the whole of our
conversation, "so then, you can manage to
look at everything in life as an object of observation and severe minute analysis?"

"Yes, I can.   Predominance of the think-

ing over the emotional faculties is a characteristic of my brain."

"Don't you consider this a disadvantage to
you? Such constant vigilance must deprive
you of all directness in feeling."

"To some extent, yes. But this want of
directness is fully compensated by the very
process of observation and analysis, which are
a source of intense pleasure to me. Besides,
in the place of mere intensity of impression,
I attain a far wider range; for my mind has
the pleasure of perceiving and discriminating
certain nice shades, which escape the notice
of others."

A smile rises to Roslawski's lips, and I feel
my soul freezing within me.

And now, summer is dead and gone: withered with suffering and desire, the flame-red
flower of Life has fallen to the ground. Now
once more the infinite ice-plains are stretching all around me. Behold the sun quenched
in the black sky, and the greenish Northern
Lights rising above the horizon. And my ice-
cold dreams, that had died, now come to life
again. And see! that Soul of mine, which
trampled my flowers beneath her feet, girds
up her loins and goes forth into the snowy

Infinite, priding herself upon her sorry triumph, and singing joyously her lofty and sublime hymn to Death!

Oh, how terrible it is, when the Soul is victorious! How terrible!

The weather has changed very suddenly; it is nearly as warm as in summer, and the leaves seem to have turned yellow with heat.

I am coming home from the office, alone and forsaken by all.

I am dreaming (like a dream indeed it is) of the boundless fields, the picturesque ridges, the dark forests and fragrant meadows of Klosow. I see the park, too, with its neatly-trimmed shrubberies and lofty trees; their bare trunks and leafy tops forming a canopy high overhead under the sky, and the foliage turning yellow or red in the sunny glare. The pond, too, do I see—so large that it may be called a lake—the pond, bleak and desolate in the moonless, starless night; that night, when I broke away from the magic spell of Life, and slew my own felicity with my own hands.

Before my eyes, people are walking along the avenues, strewn with dry dead leaves. The slightest breath of air brings down from the trees these tatters and strips, once a purple kingly mantle: but men go on, pitilessly trampling down the rustling leaves.

Now I am in a strange humour—a sort of Pantheistic mood. My Ego is multiplying, growing into countless gods, and penetrating the whole world, wherein there is no room for aught save Me. And, therefore, prodigious amazement takes hold of me, when I think how all these crowds of people can tread upon my golden autumnal leaves, or glance at me, because I have a noticeable face and a hat *à la diable m'enporte*. Can I think that they live? There is no life but mine only.

No, they have not life.

And there,—an immense way off, on the farther shore of the Ocean of Infinity,—there he stands, he, the only foe worthy of me: and he waits that I should go onward to meet him!

And I—I stand in fear. For a week I have not been at Obojanski's, where he goes pretty nearly every night.

When the thought comes to me of the splendid sorrel mount I had, and of Janusz whose lips were so sweet, I have a mind to burst out crying. But I shall not go back there, unless . . . Oh, if I could help going back!

I have an irresistible inclination to seek for types amongst people. I do not like things accidental, either without logical connection, or without connection with the special nature of a given mind. If it depended upon me, I would, like a scientist at work in his laboratory, remove from every character whatever is unnecessary and unessential, lest this should render its reactions with others too complicated and obscure. For example, I should like to make of Obojanski a sage of ancient Greece, and eliminate from him everything that disagreed with this type. Smilowicz should be a narrow-minded Socialist: as matters stand, he is too clever for his type, and most needlessly cleverer than Obojanski. Roslawski is almost perfect. I should only desire—and this, too, for purely personal motives—that he might look upon marriage from a less absolutely ideal standpoint.

What my own type is, I do not know. Very likely I have none; and this has troubled my mind for ever so many a year. I am unable to find anything general in myself, or to define my own nature in one word and make an abstraction of it. For that, I am far too complex.

My father was a bricklayer; and yet there is nothing vulgar in my face or postures or motions. I sweep my floor and clean my own shoes: yet my hands are as soft as velvet. During the whole of my childhood, I used either to go barefoot, or in cheap, clumsy boots; yet my feet are white, and bear no mark that I ever went so. My work for the greater part of the day—the adding up of innumerable columns of figures—is such as might benumb most brains, and yet I am quite able to think keenly. Though I neither write poetry, nor sing, nor paint, I have a thoroughly artistic mind. My way of living borders on the penurious; yet I have all the epicurean instincts of those who live at another's expense. After all, I am (as I am perfectly well aware) nothing extraordinary; and yet, to be the little that I am, I have not undergone one twinge of conscience; in all that is Me, there is not one atom of harm done to any one, and no one single tear of any being alive.

A post-card from Martha, with a "Decadent" figure of a woman, all covered over with microscopic handwriting.

"Grandfather is dangerously ill. I have

not had a wink of sleep for a week, and am
almost light-headed in consequence. Nervous energy alone has sustained me till now:
I cannot answer for the morrow. I continually feel as if my brain were swelling, and
would presently fly to pieces. I am tormented
with the horrible uselessness of undeserved
pain. I don't want to think what the end of
all this is to be. I only know that something
within me is giving way. Never yet has my
spirit been so broken down: I am now paying
the score of the Past, and with usurious interest besides. The autumn of life has come
upon me, taking me unawares: nor is it re-
lieved by any reminiscence of a spring-time
that never was mine. Every night, and all
night long, I am sitting by poor Grandfather's bed, going over my interminable
litany of sorrow, and shedding my heart's
blood drop by drop.—M."

And about Janusz not one word!

As I am going home from the office to-day,
I come across Smilowicz, with a big parcel of
books under his arm. In spite of his ridiculous smile, the man impresses me: the life he
leads is in such strict conformity with the doc-

trines which he professes. Obojanski tells me
he is a very able teacher of Natural Science;
but he loses all his lessons, because he cannot
reconcile his advanced opinions with what the
school superintendents require. For some
time past, he has had nothing, or nearly nothing, to eat: he spends his mornings in the University Library, and his evenings at Obojanski's.

As we pass along by the "Philharmonia"
building, he informs me that he has never
been inside it.

"Do you object to going there?"

"Most certainly. I am against music, fine
costumes, everything that represents satisfaction and amusement. To me all that only suggests extortion, wrong-doing, and injustice:
for but a few are able to go there, and that
only at the expense of others."

"But you forget that wrong-doing and injustice are by no means essentials of the Beautiful, of Art, and of artistic delight, though
at the present time they happen to exist in
connection with these. Your theory seems to
me to make far too much of what actually *is*.
Try to deliver yourself from the fetters of
the Temporal; look upon the present day, as

being yourself outside of it and soaring above
it: do you see what I mean?—I also resent
whatever is unjust, but I can separate the
Beautiful therefrom and love it, both in Art
and in life."

"Well, you may be right, but I cannot take
up so objective a point of view. In me indignation overbears any gentler artistic sentiment. Yet more: I think it is not now the
time to enjoy Art, or to plunge into the deep
and subtle analyses of Estheticism. What we
want at the present time is Action."

"But, for myself, I quiet my conscience with
the fact, which I know to be true, that I am
living now just as I should live in that future
when, as Ferri says, all are from the very outset to have equal opportunities for their development."

Smilowicz is pleased.

"Ah, then you understand. . . . I was
afraid you had been surprised at my friendship for Obojanski, seeing the way I am accustomed to talk. But, you know, if scientific
work were properly remunerated, Obojanski's monographs would bring him in enough
money to live as sumptuously as he is doing
now. So he arrives at the very same result,

though by different roads. Yet that, unfortunately, is paltering with principles."

Oh, I should not object, so far as I am concerned, to any such "paltering!" As things stand, I am working too much: I might work less and do something better. . . . All my talent is quite thrown away on those everlasting accounts.

My dream is now, how to make more money. And this renders me somewhat uneasy; perhaps it is on account of pecuniary circumstances that I am now considering the possibility of marriage with Janusz, in case Roslawski . . .

This I should not like. Not because it would show my character in an ignoble light. That's nonsense. No, but it would mark how little I care for the creature I could take on such terms.

I am of those whose sin is greater than the sin of Eve and Adam: I have eaten of the fruit of the knowledge that there is neither good nor evil.

Yes, for I have gone on—on to the very end. Every one has something he can call his own. Sufferers magnify in their mind the power of

suffering; those who have abandoned everything make a god of their strength of will to
do so. But I have nothing left, nothing absolutely. Of beauty I have not enough to love
that beauty in myself. Wisdom is wisdom
from one standpoint only: that lost, its very
idea ceases to exist. I have too much mind
to be artful and mysterious, so I strike no one
as being uncommon. I have all the short-
comings of a perfect sage; for I believe in
nothing, and am indifferent to all things. But
I am not, as sages are, encyclopædic, nor do
I love knowledge, nor have I any. At the
same time, I do not, like a typical Decadent,
hug myself at the thought of my doubts and
of my indifference. Quite the contrary—to
others, nay, even to myself, I play the part of
one that is blithe, well-favoured, happy, and
quite satisfied with being what I am. This
is not because I deliberately try to keep my
secret to myself, but because merriment is to
my mind less wearisome than the apathy of
doubt. And I have not as my own even
what I say here, for I am not sure that it is
true. . . .

Roslawski . . . ? Well, say I am attracted
by the interest of an experiment.

Out of which I am making a grave and important affair, simply because of my love for some pathos in life. . . .

Why, Janusz himself can be "distinguished" on certain occasions.

Madame, (he writes),
May I venture to remind you that the period chosen by you, within which to give me a definite answer, will have come to an end on Monday next?
I beg to remain, Madame,
Most respectfully yours,
Janusz.

Yes, the time has come. I shall go to Obojanski's to-night.

Here I have come, with fevered lips and ice-cold heart, only to find that Roslawski went away but a quarter of an hour ago, having to dine with some friends this evening.

I still can smell in the air the brand of cigars that he smokes. . . . My eye-brows and lids are twitching as if agitated by some witch's spell.

Yet I experience not the least disappointment at not finding him here: rather a sense of relief, that I can put the affair off a little longer.

Obojanski tells me what a favourite of Roslawski I am, and goes so far as to hint—in jest—that he is in love with me. This very evening he was asking why I have paid no visit to my old Professor for such a length of time. This, for a man of his sort, must mean a great deal.

In the main, however, Obojanski is this evening in a pessimistic and quarrelsome mood. He blames me for too readily taking up with new trends of thought: which does me great harm. There is no contemporary poet equal to Homer: I ought therefore to be somewhat more deeply read in the works of the old classics, which reflect such a healthy feeling of harmony between body and mind.

"You are," he says, "daily less mindful of the admirable maxim, 'Mens sana in corpore sano.'"

"Why, no; I decidedly uphold proper care of the body, to make it hardy and healthy, and able to resist the wear and tear of our now over-subtle and over-sensitive minds."

"Yes, but nowadays our very minds are diseased."

"Well, then, let my motto be: 'In a sound body, a diseased mind!'"

Or what people may choose to call diseased.

Scholars and thinkers, though they surely must have made some studies in logic, yet reason thus by analogy: Disease of the body is any departure from its normal state: *consequently,* any but an average mind is diseased. But if they start from the premise that mind and body are identical, then why reason at all on the matter?

Now I would burst into song, to run about in the open country, flooded with the white low sunbeams, and to utter cries of joy.

Why? Because the old Professor has said: "He is in love with you!" And because I believe he has spoken the truth.

Yes, and I shall continue to believe it till sundown, and I still am dreaming of a joyful triumph. I had one before, but it was far from joyful.

To-morrow evening I shall go to see Obojanski once more; and I shall tremble with great fear.

I am sure my answer to Janusz will be delayed. To-night Smilowicz and Roslawski accompanied me home together. I cannot say whether I shall get any opportunity for a private talk with him. Perhaps it is better so: but, then, Janusz is waiting for his answer down in Klosow.

Roslawski is the one man in the world before whose gaze my eyes must droop. That alone can throw me off my balance, rob me of my customary untroubled assurance; for it is the only force able to master mine.

Towards the end, our talk turns to love and marriage.

The latter Smilowicz looks upon from an economic standpoint, and thinks it is, in our present conditions of life, a necessary evil. All the same, he informs Obojanski that a certain mutual acquaintance of theirs, who married not long ago, is perfectly happy with his wife.

"Ah, yes," Obojanski guardedly observes, "in the first months, even such a thing is not impossible."

Roslawski's face puts on a cold smile. Indeed, he is in favour of marriage, as is quite natural with a man who has sown his wild oats, and is desirous of love that is lawful. The fastest men I ever knew were theoretically in favour of monogamy. Imszanski, too, always told Martha that, were it not for the fickleness of women and various other untoward conditions, he would be happiest with one woman and one alone.

On this point, Obojanski is a sceptic; this is the only subject on which he can speak wittily.

"And you,—do you intend to marry for love?" Roslawski asks me suddenly, with a subtle tinge of flippancy in his tone, such as men of his kind always use in speaking to women: an attitude with him quite instinctive and unreasoned, since he is very far from sharing Obojanski's prejudice concerning the inferiority of our sex.

A sudden qualm of terror seizes me, but I master it, and say with a tranquil smile: "Your question makes me feel as if under examination. Confess now that you are at present wanting to know what my reply will be, not what I really intend to do."

There is an ironical gleam in his eyes.

"You may take my word for it that I am not," he answers emphatically.

"In that case, I'll tell you as much as I myself know. If I marry for love, it will not last very long; if, on the contrary, I do so with judgment and out of a conscious conviction that the man is destined for me, then I shall be faithful to my husband all my life."

"And which of these alternatives do you prefer?"

"The second," I reply; and add truthfully, "for there are certain classes of feeling in which I object to changes."

"Really? But you would have the same result, even if you married for love."

"I am afraid I cannot bring myself to believe in the eternal duration of mere feeling. Love in marriage, as a rule, becomes in time a sort of mutuality of habit, a sense of solidarity, as it were, and now and then even a brotherhood of minds. It is just in such cases that divorce would be advisable."

"And when it is a marriage of reason?"

"Why, then the question is correctly stated from the first; at the outset, suitability of characters and of individualities are taken into consideration, so as to prevent any possibility of future disagreement."

"And yet it is possible to obtain the continuance of love by incessantly watching over it, by not unfrequently putting on a mask, and by keeping private certain emotions and states of mind which might prejudice one party in the eyes of the other."

How the remembrance of Janusz comes back to me as I listen! Of all this, *he* knew nothing at all.

"I doubt whether so much trouble is very profitable," I return. "The game is hardly worth the candle."

"And yet some there are," he goes on to say, "for whom present bliss has no value, if they know beforehand that the morrow will take it away. And they often prefer to renounce it entirely."

The words are spoken calmly, without any apparent significance; yet there is in their tone, I fancy, an under-current of ominous import.

"Well," I say, repressing my irrational dread, "then let all such take care to marry with judgment."

"Nevertheless, to give love and get in its place only intellectuality is not a good bargain, I fear."

Now—*now I understand*—and I almost feel hatred for the man. Yes, I may throw myself under the wheels of a locomotive, but never will I say I do that out of love for it!

"Reasonable people should remember that 'the heart is no servant,' and that, beyond intellectual and conscious resolve, we can find nothing on which we can safely count." This I say, as light-heartedly and as smilingly as I can, feeling meanwhile the dismay of a horrible misgiving—almost a certitude—clutching at my heart.

And now at last I am alone with Roslawski and Obojanski. I remain in my corner all the evening, saying little, overwhelmed with dread of the coming decisive moment. That tall, red-haired gentleman in glasses,—I simply detest him!

Roslawski sets to playing Wagner,—stiffly, correctly, like an automaton. His playing grates strongly upon my nerves: each of the notes taps on my heart-strings.

Obojanski is enchanted. He goes about the room on tiptoe, making the floor creak as he walks; he fetches music from the book-shelves for Roslawski, and lays them in heaps on the piano. Now and again he glances at me, and whispers, almost aloud: "How very beautifull!" He finally brings me a volume of some German encyclopædia, and opens it at the article "Wagner," which he expects me to read.

I am so upset that I nearly break down. Resting my head on the back of the sofa, I look up at the ceiling to swallow down my tears as they well up. And I begin to weave fancies.

A wonderful immemorial forest, through which, clad in armour, knights are riding on white steeds. Most lofty oaks, strong-limbed and gnarled, with black trunks and dark-blue foliage, strike their roots deep into the ground. Amid mosses in hue like malachite, ferns put forth their sprays of sea-green lace. Fairies dance merrily among the trees, and scatter round them pearls of ringing laughter. And far away, lost in reverie, upon a dark, enchanted lake there floats a swan. A strange, clear, chilly splendour illuminates the twilight.

All at once a thunderbolt, a red thunderbolt falls: and the oak forest and the lake vanish into the depths of the earth. . . . Yet thunderstorms only take place on sultry summer days.

No, no, all this was but a dream.

Now there comes before me the infinite wilderness of my own ice-plains, hard-frozen beneath the cold and glassy skies. I am afraid, I am horribly afraid, I cannot breathe, seeing those endless plains of ice, under that canopy of green and frosty light: it is the kingdom of my soul!

But far away, at the sky-line, where without warmth the Aurora Borealis beams, there stands a huge statue, a basalt-hewn statue. This recks not of the unbounded wilderness, nor of the chilly gleams of the Northern Lights, nor of the stars, those silver eyes of Time. Tranquil and undismayed it stands. That is Roslawski.

On I march towards him, plodding through the deep and drifting snow; at his feet, I fall upon my knees.

And I beseech him to hide the boundless wilderness from my sight; to protect me from the icy air of death, so that I may dwell in this land of my soul, and yet not die. "For behold, this day I am weak exceedingly, this day I stand in fear of the plains of ice."

But he says: "Here in the snows around me, you must first lay out a garden as of the tropics; and yourself must blossom into a flame-red and purple rose."

And I make answer: "My lord, without the light of the sun, how is any rose to blow?"

Once more a thunderclap resounds. He is gone. I am all alone amid my ice-plains: and I live yet.

Bound I am, with fetters made of ice. The silvery wings of my soul are glittering under the canopy of heaven, and in the greenish splendour of the Northern Lights. She would not share with me my years of burning heat, and now she will not have me share this realm of hers. A snake is lying on my bosom, and, coiled about my neck, sucks the warm blood thence. . . .

We bid good-night to Obojanski, and go out into the street together.

"I have to tell you something; or, rather, I have one question, only one, to put to you." These are my first words.

"I am quite at your service."

From the instant when I begin to speak, the sense of dread passes away from me, and an immense quietude takes its place.

"I must, however, lay down one condition. I will have from you no other answer save.

the word *Yes* or *No*. I do not wish—and this
is of consequence to me—to hear any comments whatever. Do you agree?"

"Most willingly," he returns, with a smile;
"the condition that you lay down I certainly
shall keep."

"You must know then," I go on, "that, since
I became acquainted with you, I have known
you for the only man who could make me
happy. Some time ago, another man, one who
deserves my sympathy and whom I trust,
asked me to marry him. Being of opinion
that, in the last resort, the knowledge that one
is greatly loved may serve as a substitute for
happiness, I have taken a month to think the
matter over. My decision depends upon your
answer. I ought perhaps to add that I can
foresee what this is likely to be; but that I am
very anxious to get absolute certainty on this
point, lest I should at some future time have
to reproach myself with having let my chance
of happiness go by."

There is a silence.

"May I venture to ask you to put your question in a more definite form?"

"Are you, or are you not, willing to marry
me?"

Another silence.

"No: and yet, supposing that . . ."

"Remember my condition."

No more is said.

In front of my lodgings we bid each other a calm and friendly farewell.

The next morning, on my way to my office, I put a long scented envelope into a post-box. It is addressed to Janusz.

Nevertheless, the decision which it contains is—not to marry him.

Yes, I am now the bond-slave of my soul: these my ice-plains, it is no longer mine to leave them.

I have done with suffering. . . . During all these long days and nights, I have not shed one tear. I do not suffer now: the agony-delirium has passed those limits, beyond which no difference is felt between joy and misery, beyond which there is no night of woe, that contrasts with day.

In the still autumn twilight, I am shut up in my dark and lonely room. Lest I should awake my soul, that has fallen asleep, I am pacing the soft carpet with noiseless steps.

I am in terror of the very movements which

I myself make. Trembling with cold—or is it with my own emptiness of heart?—and leaning against my doorway in the darkness, wrapped in the folds of my soft shaggy portière, I open my swooning lips to utter a soundless cry, and look staring into the mobile fluttering dark with tired and quiet gaze.

I do not suffer; I exist—in a world wherein the night of woe no longer is a contrast with day, wherein there prevails a tranquil dusk, without sun and without stars.

There is no Ego of mine. I am beyond existence and beyond nothingness—in that world wherein dies the immemorial conflict between dream and vigil; where Wrong, robed in her queenly purple, is no longer shadowed by Vengeance, in her pallid green attire; where stony Hatred no longer hugs in her fierce embrace the weeping god of love; where the marble statue of Pride no longer renders homage to the grim spectre, Fear; wherein there are no more wretched victories, nor the portentous delights of worshipping oneself and the Power of Self!

No, there is no more any Ego of mine. . . . I am in a world to which even the unlimited fields of Infinity cannot reach, for it

was everlastingly beyond all limits. I am in
a world in which Duration neither flows nor
stands still; wherein Solitude is not, though
neither are there spirits to commune with;
where there is only no solitude, because there
is no Me.

Do I suffer? No. I am in a world where
I have no being.

I could well die, if I chose: but my body,
well-favoured as it is, would fain not part
from my bright, though mournful soul.
Therefore am I willing to live.

But there is nought for which I can any
longer care; I dwell in a world which my soul
is never to behold: for when Death comes,
my soul's existence will be over.

Yet not because nothingness is *there*. To
believe that *there* is nothingness, one must indeed have an intense power of faith. I cannot
bring myself to accept the creed of nothingness. For in the world where I am now,
neither Being is, nor Non-Being; there is
neither the Ego nor the Non-Ego; nor has the
soul ever laid her icy hand upon the body:
I am in a world wherein there is no soul of
mine.

My soul will end its being at the instant of

Death, not because that world is a world of nothingness, but because therein is no such thing as indestructibility of substance.

I might, if I chose, die; but death matters nothing to me. To solve the riddle of life, I do not require death. For now I know all. I know that, in that other world, knowledge and ignorance are not incompatible, nor is there in that world any desire to know. And therefore I shall never solve the riddle of life, because I have solved it now.

I know that which no man knows: that to read the riddle, I need not know all things. For there is no Me!

And I am indeed in a world which contradicts our world, but with a contradiction in which negation and assertion are the same.

But in one thing I do believe—the only thing that is.

And that thing is: *No!*

Such a *No* as does not contradict *Yes,* but means what *No* means, taken together with *Yes.*

Such a *No* as Roslawski said to me.

And if I suffer nothing, it is because I belong to a world wherein joy and sorrow are the same.

II

THE "GARDEN OF RED FLOWERS"

IMSZANSKI was patient and persevering,
and determined to take no repulse as final.
In the end he had the good luck to come at
the right time, when Martha was in a favour-
able mood: whereupon she relented, gave up
all her objections, and married him very willingly.

For close on a year after their marriage, I
had no sight of them. They were travelling
about Europe, and Martha had never been
abroad. Every two or three days I would get
a post-card from her, which I of course "read
between the lines." Plunged though she was
in an atmosphere of intense bliss, she was continually revolving the thought of death in her
mind. But that is probably no unfrequent
phenomenon in such cases.

She returned, bringing with her a son a few
months of age—returned very pale, and like

a shadow, yet prettier than she had ever been before.

Having grown much thinner, she seems to be taller now. She wears her dark plaited hair round her tiny head, like a crown. Her age is thirty or thereabouts. Imszanski, though considerably older, seems of that age too.

They have rented a flat in Warsaw, and insisted on my sharing it with them. But I spend the best part of my day in the office, just as in former times.

To me, life brings nothing new; my memories are mostly colourless or grey. Truly, I am disappointed with myself, since I belong to the class of those who "give great promise" all their life.

All the same, though I cannot overcome this, my "tristesse de vivre," I daily look upon it with more indifferent serenity.

You at first look straight in front of you. Then, when a certain point has been passed, you begin to look behind you. Now, this point is by no means the instant when happiness passes you by, or you are struck some awful blow, waking you up from a sweet illusion; it is a moment which may, like every other, go by in laughter or in tears: it may even be slept through; and you do not know when it comes, but you know well enough when it has passed.

For me, it has passed: and now I look behind me. Though I should prefer to look nowhere at all. I look back, and I think all that was perhaps not worth such a fuss. . . . And yet! . . .

In any case, I have learned some wisdom, and wisdom is eternal. There remains of it enough for me to smile in my solitude. And there remains some pride, too,—the pride of knowing that I am what I am.

On returning from a concert, I went with my friend, Wiazewski, to Lipka, to meet the company we usually see there.

I take some interest in the atmosphere, reeking and tainted though it is, of a high-class restaurant, crowded with "gilded youth," old financiers, beautiful actresses, and *demi-mondaines*. The saloon is a large one, lit with wide-branched chandeliers. The air is thick with tobacco-smoke, through which the sparkles of a thousand lights and the brilliant notes of the merry orchestra assail both eye and ear. The ceiling is painted in antique style. The background is all speckled with bright stains—blots of white napery on the tables, and candles shaded with glass "lampions" of various tints, forming spots of many a colour. There is a twinkling mingled with a tinkling: the rays of electric blossoms over our heads, and around us the jingling of cups and glasses, join together in a seething tumult.

This is a life apart. Not the daily round of appearances—the mere mask which hides life,—but life immediate, naked, real. You see here that in spite of all it is possible to be merry and to care for nothing. Here are no unsightly garments, no clumsy inartistic motions; no children (that most objectionable element in life!); no "respectable" women, who are to be recognized by their ugliness, their want of style and charm, their tediousness and stupidity, and the fact that, when they think at all, they are always hopelessly depressed. This is a very good illustration of the "Law of Selection": in marriage, the qualities of virtue and fidelity are of more account as guarantees of felicity than such endowments as beauty and health. Beautiful women of a lively temperament are set aside as too knowing, too exacting, and of doubtful trustworthiness: and so they go to swell the ranks of the fallen.

For my own part, did I not fear the accusation of anti-social tendencies, I would, from the height of my cheerless philosophical eminence, declare that I view the "frail sisterhood," as an institution, without intolerance. Therein breathes something that tells of times gone by: something existing, but of which men do not speak. There exist human beings, scorned as a class, whatever their personal endowments may be, with whom no other class is allowed to come in contact, under pain of defilement:—not unlike pariahs. These beings are to be bartered for precious metals by means of a secret contract—bought as the slaves of ancient times were bought. Their existence is kept a secret quite disinterestedly, for the mere sake of the secret itself: every one knows all about them. In our days, so hyper-civilized, so deprived of all poetry by reason of excessive culture, this is a most astonishing state of things.

Nearly every man here present has a wife, actual or intended: but these are not permitted to enter: they would be by far too much out of place.

No doubt, their wives, having put the children to bed, had some words with the servant over the daily account of money spent, and put on a clean night-gown (of a wretchedly bad cut, by the way), say their prayers and lay themselves down to sleep under the red woolen coverlet, thinking all the time: "How late he always returns after these meetings!" or else she may bite her nails with fury, revolving in her mind the idea of another angry scene with her husband—a scene foredoomed as heretofore to be without effect. Or again, in agonized resignation, she may bend over the baby's cradle, and murmur mournfully, with naïve pathos: "For your sake, my child!" And the girls whose troths are plighted have long ago gone to sleep under the wing of their domestic guardians, lulled to slumber with some such sweet fancies as: "Most men have intrigues before they marry: he, and he alone, has surely none." And so forth. . . .

They are foolish—but fortunate, because not allowed to come in here.

Ah! once upon a time, in the days of my childish marvellings, how bitterly did I weep over all these things!

"Stephen, how late is it?" I asked Wiazew-ski.

"It will soon be midnight. Our friends are not coming, it would seem. Are you in a hurry to get home?"

"I never am; I have got a latch-key, and so wake nobody when I come in. But are you not yourself sometimes engaged of an evening?"

He shook his head, his teeth shining good-humouredly in a friendly smile.

"You know perfectly well that there is not an assignation I would not set aside to spend an evening with you. To me, friendship is a boon far rarer and far more precious than love."

"I do not hold with you at all. I have enough of the cold consideration granted me by the world."

Stephen smiled again.

"There is no help for it, Janka," he said. "Men of our times are too weakly to love an all-around woman: the very thought of one gives them an unpleasant shock. The day for types of women so extremely complex as you are has now gone by; at present women are preferred who display some very distinct and special characteristic: especially either primitive natures, or such as have been depraved by civilization; or types of spirituality or of sensuality; women either of very well-balanced minds, or nervous even to hysteria; or, again, those in whom warmth of heart or a distinguished bearing prevails. And that is why the monogamic instinct is now dying out completely: in a few years' time, it will be no more."

Wiazewski was on the war-path, the topic being a favourite one of his.

"For how can a man be true to his wife, if he takes her 'for better, for worse, . . . till death do them part,' only, let us say, to kiss a mole that she has on her neck, just under her left ear? Monogamy requires exceedingly strong, rich, abundant natures."

"Then it would follow that our near future would witness our return to the hetairism of primæval times?"

"No doubt; for both the primitive instincts of the senses, and their ultra-refined activity, have identically the same result."

A handsome woman, with strikingly original features, accompanied by an elderly man, clean-shaven (an actor probably) went by near our table. She too had the look of an actress.

Wiazewski's eyes followed her with keen scrutiny.

"A fine woman," I remarked.

He turned his eyes away from her.

"She is not my sort," he replied. "Far too cultured for my taste."

Then he again returned to the subject.

"Hetairism, yes. Yes, undoubtedly. But if it all depended upon me, I should wish for one slight restriction. . . . You see, one of the most genial types of womanhood is the *wifely* type: that of a woman faithful, trustworthy, absolutely your own. . . . It were desirable that such a type should not perish entirely. But I should wish her only as a class to contrast with others, and as a haven of rest, when wearied with those."

I was gazing at the pretty Frenchwoman; suddenly I saw a delighted expression flash over her striking and reposeful face, somewhat harem-like in its beauty. I instinctively followed her glance, and—not without somewhat of embarrassed astonishment—discovered Imszanski. He was just entering from the doorway, and going through the saloon, distributing on all sides bows or smiles, as a beautiful woman does flowers. His wonderfully sweet and dreamy eyes were seeking some one in the room.

A sudden flash lit them up, as they met the gaze of the handsome Frenchwoman.

Imszanski, on his way to them, happened to see me, and Wiazewski in my company.

Directly, and without showing the least surprise or embarrassment, he changed his expression and saluted us with urbane cordiality, and though he had just gone past our table, he returned, shook hands, and begged leave to sit down beside us.

The Frenchwoman at the neighbouring table was just putting on her gloves, while the actor paid the bill. I should very willingly have told Imszanski not to mind about us, but go on to his acquaintances, who we could see were expecting him. But I refrained, not wishing to lay on his shoulders a burden of gratitude for keeping this matter concealed from Martha, which might later have proved irksome to him.

Stephen, too, understood.

"We are here," he presently said, "waiting for Madame Wildenhoff, Owinski with his intended, and Czolhanski. It is rather late now: I doubt whether they are going to turn up."

Imszanski turned aside to say something to a waiter, when he noted with satisfaction that the actors had left the saloon.

He then said he hoped and trusted that we would not look upon him as an intruder, though he had thrust himself on us in such a way.

Czolhanski, a journalist, arrived at about one o'clock, together with Owinski and his fianceé, Miss Gina Wartoslawska, whom I had seen several times previously at Imszanski's.

Her real name is Regina; but she is called Gina. In the movements of her lithe elastic figure is a sort of snake-like suppleness, which tells us of a nervous nature, burning with a passion almost painfully suppressed. She is like a tame panther. Her eyes, long, narrow, partly concealed beneath thin lids, wander hither and thither about the floor with a drooping, apathetic look. Her lips are broad, flattened as it were by many kisses, moist and crimson as if they bled. And, with all that, there is in her something of the type of a priestess.

She came in, drawing black gloves off her slender hands, greeted us with an unsmiling face, and at once called out to a waiter who was passing by:

"A glass of water!"

She drank the whole glass at one draught, and sat down at some distance from the table, with her head bent forward, and her hands clasped over her knees. Owinski took a seat close beside her.

"Czolhanski," he told us, "has only just got through his critique of the leading actress in to-night's play. We had to stay for him in the editor's waiting-room."

"Ah," grumbled the critic, "it's beastly, this work all done to order and at railway speed! Such a piece as that ought to be thought over till it is possible to form a definite judgment upon it. As it is, we are forced to save the situation by means of a lot of sententious generalities."

At last, Madame Wildenhoff arrived with her husband. At the unexpected sight of Imszanski in our company, a deep blush mantled her face. She seated herself next to Gina, and burst into a fit of chuckling, shading her eyes with beautiful hands that carried many

a ring. All this was rather unusual and disquieting. Imszanski flushed slightly; a warm
haze, so thin that it could scarce be seen, bedimmed his eyes, and his long lashes drooped
over them.

Wildenhoff, an unpleasant cut-and-dried
sort of man, whose humour inclined to sarcastic silence, proposed that we should pass
into a private room. She protested.

"Oh, no! I dearly love noise and music and
an uproar all about me. We had better stay
here, hadn't we?"

Wildenhoff smiled at his wife and was presently deep in study of the bill of fare.

She again set to laughing without any
cause: a disquieting sort of chuckle, with
something like a sob now and then.

I glanced at the two couples, feeling a
twinge of envy. "There is love between
them." . . .

Oh, but all that was so very, very long ago!

I wish Stephen would fall in love with me.
But he is always running after some theory or
other. At times he is as droll as a boarding-
school girl. I do believe his friendship for
me to be absolutely disinterested. He, on his
side, declares that a handsome woman, as such,

means nothing to him. The type he loves is uncultured, shallow-brained animality.

He is as yet too youthful. Men's taste for women more spiritualized, more cultured, more quick-witted, is only a reaction: it shows a decline in the vital forces, and tells of old age about to set in.

All the time of our return home, he, rather in the clouds, holds forth with artificial animation.

"With you, Janka, I could well live alone in a wilderness, were you even twice as beautiful as you are—and never remember that I was in presence of a being of the other sex. And, indeed, this is the most natural thing in the world: if such a thought ever entered my brain, I should feel humiliated that a woman was mentally my equal."

"But is it with perfect disinterestedness that you have chosen a pretty young woman for your best friend?"

"Why should I not do so? That gives me the advantage of a double pleasure: not only can I enjoy your conversation; I can enjoy your appearance as well."

"You might just as easily take a handsome man for your friend."

"Yes, but then beauty in a woman generally accompanies intelligence; whereas good-looking men are, as a rule, rather foolish. Moreover, however objectively I strive to judge of things, I must confess that a woman's body is more handsome than a man's."

"And what of her mind?"

"Why, she has none: I mean there is no such thing as a feminine mind. Though, look you, it is not unlikely that women also have minds. There is nothing sexual about the brain, either way."

"Yet you have always said I had the mind of a man."

"I was wrong; as a friend, you are neither male nor female. You are something that I set in a class apart; and I want you to do the same by me."

At our door, I take leave of the whole company. Imszanski desires to go on with "the ladies" a little farther, but he is back at once. I can guess why. . . .

The Imszanskis are, as they have given out, "At Home" on Sundays. From three till dinner-time, the door is practically open to all. These "At Homes" are formal, tedious, and rather pretentious affairs. There are, besides, but few people who come; for Imszanski has no acquaintances with whom he is on really cordial terms.

But I like these Sundays: they soothe my nerves as warm baths do. With the people who come, I need not attempt to keep up any appearance of truthfulness. On the contrary, I say very far-fetched and most fantastic things—things, besides, that I know not to be likely to interest any one present.

But here is the field wherein Imszanski bears away the palm. Never are his movements more elegant, his smiles more cordial, his glances more winning. No one can better than he deal out the small change of social amenities in his looks, his superficial judgments on literature and on art; none, when addressing a compliment to a woman, can more subtly envelope what he means in a mist of allusions.

Both husband and wife appear to advantage. He, with the perfect culture of his ancient and noble descent, is simply enchanting. Martha is a contrast to him, as standing for something newer, but deeper: the culture given by unassuageable sorrow, the concentrated reverie seen in the sad looks of those dark-blue eyes, albeit a kind smile always flutters on her parched red lips.

Now and again, the Wildenhoffs come here on Sundays. They produce a most interesting effect. Everybody is saying that Madame has an intrigue with Imszanski. Martha knows that, and every one knows that Martha knows: and she feigns ignorance, though aware that no one believes her. So here is being piled up an immense heap of lies: which is a curious situation, and as such not unpleasing to me.

Of Madame Wildenhoff, Lombroso would have said that she belonged to the class of courtesans "by right of birth." Her snowy flesh, her golden hair, her brows, blackly looming above azure eyes, her rosy cheeks and scarlet mouth,—the whole of this fairy colouring gives an appearance of complete artificiality; and her wonderful shape and inborn talent for coquetry make one regret that such gifts should have been lost on such a very unsuitable field of action. For I myself have not the least doubt that need of money is but a secondary motive with those who join the "frail sisterhood." Were it, as is generally supposed, the chief inducement, what should force men to lead lives so similar to the lives of demi-mondaines?

I like to watch Imszanski with her, playing the part of the host. Nothing, it would seem, nothing in the whole world can possibly throw him off his balance. He greets her just as he would any other visitor, with a set "So-pleased-to-meet-you" sort of smile; gives her as much of his time as he does to any of the women there; and converses with her, partly flirting, partly freezing her with the haughty consciousness of his preëminence as a drawing-room "lion." He makes no endeavour to conceal his liking for her, but shows just as much as it becomes him to have for any young and handsome woman. It would be a breach of the laws of hospitality, if he had not for each of these a few discreet compliments, and for each a look of warm admiration, beaming from those ever half-curtained almond eyes.

Orcio is sometimes called in from the nursery; and in he comes—a little fair-haired boy in black velvet, with a superb collar of yellowish lace. The ladies talk to him in French, in order to praise his accent.

To-day the following conversation took place:

"*Qui aimes-tu davantage, Georges,—papa ou maman?*" was the question put to him by Madame Wildenhoff, who, her hand in a white glove of Danish leather, was stroking the boy's curls with a blandishing smile.

"*C'est papa,*" was Orcio's reply.

"*Et pourquoi donc?*"

"*Parce que maman ne rit jamais.*"

Whereupon everybody set hurriedly to expatiate upon the accomplishments of Orcio,—who is not yet four! This they did, wishing to hide a certain confusion felt: that *enfant terrible* had so unconsciously touched on a matter that every one knew, but no one talked about.

Madame Wildenhoff, who no doubt expected the boy's answer, and had perhaps elicited it purposely, was the only person to underline its meaning; she let her long eyelashes droop over her rosy cheeks, pretending to be shocked at the unseemly associations that it had by her means called up.

Martha laughed in merry contradiction of what Orcio had just said; then, kissing his fair brow, she told him to make a nice bow

to the company and go back to the nursery
with the maid.

Society is irksome to Martha now. We two
often went together formerly to the theatre or
to a concert: at present she cares no more to
go.

I mostly spend my evenings with her, in
interminable conversations. She either relates
something to me, or else she "gives sorrow
words." I listen.

She is just now much grieved that her husband Witold has for nearly a fortnight hardly
ever been at home. Some days we even dine
without him.

"It is surely so," she was saying yesterday.
"He enjoys his manhood to the full: everything is his. There, he has 'Bohemian' society, revelling, fast people, singing, champagne, flowers, and forgetfulness: here, he
finds the pure and quiet light of the domestic
fireside, the delights of fatherhood, the love
of a faithful wife. When he is tired of one
sort of pleasure, why then he tries the other.
. . . And *we*—we are all crippled, helpless
things—all!"

Silence for a moment.

"There he gets his amusement at the expense of those poor weaklings, whose souls have been wrenched away from them, who have lost the feeling of their human dignity, the consciousness of their right to live, even the very sense of pleasure; who groan under that most unjust burden, their own self-contempt; who feel the continual oppression of a guilt which does not exist, and for whom the first wrinkle is as a sentence of death.

"But on his domestic hearth there beams another fire, and beams on another kind of weakling; a strange creature, now no longer able to descend into Life's hurly-burly; for whom certain deeds, for many a century regarded with scorn, have through long heredity of atavistic feelings become really loathsome. . . .

"Our duty is to amuse *them*—the lords of life and death—with the effects of contrast; that *they* may have the assurance of having experienced the whole gamut of emotions, that they may enjoy their manhood to the full."

When Witold came home to-day from the club (which was at about noon) Martha received him in a beautiful white *peignoir,* trimmed with Angora fur, and asked him whether he had yet breakfasted. He thanked her graciously, kissed her hand and brow, and desired to see Orcio.

Martha changed colour. She is not so jealous, even of women, as she is of her beautiful little boy, perhaps because he is with her constantly.

The nursemaid brought Orcio, who at once jumped on to his father's knee, and began talking at the top of his voice about a number of things which had happened to interest him since the day before.

Imszanski was enchanted with the little one, and kissed his rosy face.

For men like him, there is something incomparably sublime and public-spirited in the fact of being a father; this they hold to be the only thing that compensates and atones for the life they lead.

Martha shrank away; standing at a distance, fury in her heart and a smile on her face, she looked on at the father caressing his boy.

"Look, you," she whispered to me, "this— this is my vocation, this the mission of my life; all the pain I have undergone, all the rage of my never-ending and vain revolt, all my disappointed existence; all these have been, only that they two should sit here thus, forgetting me entirely; and that all the wrong done to me by the father should come to life again in that son of his!"

But Witold, having caressed Orcio, went to bed. Not until the evening did he wake up, fresh and hearty-looking, to dine with us, kiss Martha's hand, retail with lively wit several stories then going the round of the town, and make his way to the club once more.

In his love-affairs, Wiazewski is just as fickle and as insatiable as Imszanski; but their "spheres of influence" are different. Wiazewski has a liking for seamstresses, shop-assistants, and so forth; whereas Imszanski is specially interested in cocottes (even his intrigue with Madame Wildenhoff is a case in point). Neither of the two has any great liking for the other, in spite of their mutually courteous bearing at all times. Imszanski has against my friend that he is too democratic: whereas Wiazewski looks on Imszanski as a fool.

The latter explains his dislike for *demimondaines* thus:

"I have a great liking for misdeeds, but not when committed by professional criminals."

The art of playing with his victims has been brought by him to the acme of perfection. To this end, he employs what naturalists call "mimicry." His features being rather common, he has no trouble in putting a girl off her guard; he makes up as a commercial man, or a lackey, or a waiter; and in such parts he expresses himself most eloquently in the slang of those classes, which he has picked up to perfection.

He is a thorough expert in the art of getting into touch with the minds of such people; and the ease with which he finds his way through a labyrinth of ideas quite unknown to us is truly admirable.

On principle, he is for continual change; but latterly he has been making an exception, and declares he has hit upon the right sort, or nearly so. For some time he has been "keeping company" with a girl, whom he has, on account of her exceptional qualities, distinguished from the common herd. I once saw her at his lodgings and was struck with her good looks.

He has been reading a letter from her to-day. I asked him to give it to me as a "document," which he very readily consented to do. It runs thus:

"Dear Stephen I must tell you about something that is Roman the intended husband of Genka came to see me at the shop yesterday evening and he set a-talking to me this way don't I have no notion where Genka is so I answer back what business of mine is that and he just says don't you make believe for Genka is in Krucza with that there mechanic and he keeps her I hear is in love with her but I'll pay him out for it, only the street and the number where he lives are gone clean out of my head can you tell me I know his name is Stephen and I answer this way don't you go worriting an honest fellow for he don't have nothing to say to no girls let alone such hussies as Genka he asked me where you lived and I said Krucza number 129 fourth floor and Stephen Tworkowski is your name and he said thankee and hooked it and he says he'll ask the porter in Wspolna and I said don't you poke your nose in or you'll get your head punched as you did once before when you flung dirt at me so if he comes you tell him so and give the beast a talking to. . . . And something else my dear darling ideal I write this I love you to distraction I am regularly off my head with thinking of you and I have your photo before me and kiss it night and day. O God how I love him more than my life more than my faith I can't tell what sin I have sinned that I have to pay so dear and you dearest you are so cold and you'll bring me to my grave with your coldness and in no time too I don't know but it seems to me you told Elizabeth I slept in Hoza and she makes a mock of me and I don't care a fig for I am daft for your love no one won't cure me and no one can't it's too late I loved you when I saw you first and shall till my life ends and so long as I don't put an end to it and who will make me do that but you Stephen my dearest pet and sweetheart.

"I end this scrawl of mine throwing away my pen crying my eyes out and dying of hunger for that blessed Sunday.

"Your unhappy or rather love-sick

HELA."

Quite aware that I am doing wrong, I let
Martha look back into her past; and I even
question her myself so as to bring before her
eyes the long dismal perspective of her
wounded love. I listen in the manner she
likes best, calmly and without any show of
compassion. Nor have I any for her, any
more than for a fish that must needs live in
cold water, or for a bat that cannot bear the
sunlight. Martha likes to suffer, and—perhaps for this very reason—she is compelled to
suffer. Indeed, she is something of a Sybarite
in her almost abnormal sensitiveness to pain.
She is fond of telling me all the petty foolish
troubles of an injured wife; and this procures
her an odd sense of what may be called a sort
of enjoyment.

"But, all the same, there was a time once
when he loved you, did he not?"

"Oh, Witold declares that up to now he
has loved none but me!"

"Well, well; but then at what time did *this*
—the present phase begin? For some time at
least, he must have been faithful to you."

"Oh, yes, for a few months. Quite at the
beginning. Though I myself was never
happy. . . . First of all, during the six

weeks before our wedding, I was constantly
a prey to such mystic terrors that I came near
losing my senses. You know that I do not
admit any of those hackneyed maxims of mor-
ality—and yet I continually felt that some evil
thing was afoot, and a day of reckoning close
at hand. And besides, how intolerable then
was the thought that now I *had* to marry him,
however averse I might feel to the act; that
now I had more at stake upon my side than
he on his!"

"And afterwards, by the seaside?"

"Oh, then it was entrancing! I almost felt
happy. But it lasted so short a time! Shortly
after our arrival I fell sick, and grew un-
wieldy and weakly and plain. And then, if
you can believe me, surrounded with all those
marvels of nature and of art, I was always
longing for Klosow, my own place!"

After a silence of a few minutes, she went
on:

"I saw a drawing by Brenner. It was always in my thoughts; a woman who had died
after an operation, stretched on a table, stark
and stiff. There was a man bending over her,
mourning; his hair was like Witold's. And
another picture, showing the tragedy of

motherhood: a young mother has just breathed her last; on her bosom sits a naked child, a loathsome idiot, looking out at life with wide open, bewildered, lack-lustre eyes. I can't help fancying that Orcio resembles that child."

With a sudden abrupt movement, she rang for the man-servant.

"Ask the nurse why the child is not in bed yet. I hear it making a noise. Tell her she must put it to bed. Or else take it farther away from this room."

When the servant had gone out, I said to her:

"Why, what made you speak so angrily to him."

"Really, I cannot recognize myself any more: my nerves are so horribly unstrung." . . . And she sank into a sombre reverie.

"Tell me more," I said, to draw her out.

"More? Well, I was not so badly off then. We took delight in the blue sky, in the murmuring green sea, and in our all but absolute solitude. Witold was ever by my side, tender and kind—masking with his exquisite courtesy the disgust I must have made him feel. Why, for myself I myself often felt pity and aversion; I who had never before been other than graceful all my life.

"Then things went worse. . . . Listen; but it is too much for me just now."

"Then don't talk of it, Martha."

"Ah! what does it matter after all? If I could forget . . . but I can't.

"A few weeks before George's birth, Witold for the first time spent the night away from home. I sat up all the time, and looked out through the window over the sea. Ah, that night!

"The servants had gone to bed long before. There was a great storm, with boisterous gusts of wind: and I gave ear to the never-ceasing roar of the waves. You know what a visionary I am. I at once fancied Witold must have been sailing in a boat to the farther shore of the bay, and gone down to the bottom of the sea. I was horribly alarmed for his sake; and for a time, not an inkling of the truth flashed upon my mind. The horror of my fancy came over me so strongly that I quite forgot all about his past. . . . For I believed with faith unbounded in his immense love for me, and should have scouted, as a ridiculous notion, the idea of his possibly being unfaithful. I was out of my mind with terror. I counted the hours that went by, in agonized expectation, surrounded with the dark cloudy night, and hearing the terrific howling and rolling of the winds and waves. . . . Ah, that night!

"In the morning he came in.

"With the mien of a youthful page, he doffed his hat to the ground in a courtly bow, and stood motionless in my presence, humble, clasping his hands: then, in a soft sweet voice somewhat broken by emotion, he said, in an accent of dismay:

" 'Ah! my lady, I am afraid, greatly afraid!'

" 'I did not rush to welcome him, nor did I cry out aloud: I felt too weak for any display of joy. But at that first instant, in the sole knowledge that he was living, an infinite intensity of quiet and fathomless and endless bliss flooded my heart: and I was minded to exclaim, like Mary Magdalene at the Sepulchre, 'Rabboni: which is to say, Master!'

"And then up rose the sun!

"He had never before appeared so admirable to me, as in that attitude of a page of Mediæval times, and with the playful humility of his bright smile; he had never yet been so loved by me, so dear beyond all measure. No, I had never been so glad in all my life as in this one short instant of consolation!

"And yet they say that women have intuitive minds!

"I was as it were caught and suspended in an aërial cobweb that stretched over an abyss of waters; and there I gazed upon the golden glitter of the morning landscape now that the tempest was over—gazed into the blue and shimmering stillness. Beneath me, under the bridge of hanging gossamer, rolled the sombre sea of dread and death; before me rose the sea of life, crimson and blood-red in hue. But I—I saw nothing there, save the dawn and the sunshine."

Here she broke off, closed her eyes, and, resting her head on the arm of her easy-chair, remained some time plunged in the contemplation of that past scenery, all azure and gold. I let her rest so for a while, and then, rousing her:

"Well, and what then?" said I.

She knit her brows slightly.

"Then, ah! then! It was a mere idle question, for I troubled about nothing now that I had him again; but I asked him what he had been doing all night.

" 'Oh, but I am in fear, in such fear of you,' he said, smiling, kneeling down before me, and clasping his hand—so! You know the gesture well; it is almost the embodiment of child-like humility.

" 'Oh, what?'

" 'I want you to promise you will not be angry with me.'

"I was suddenly torn with a sharp misgiving.

" 'No, do not tell me, Witold,' I whispered.

"But he was unable to conceal anything from me. All he said in excuse was that I ought to pardon everything, by reason of his great love; that no woman could ever snatch from me the place which I held in his heart. That he had not been truly unfaithful, since his true and only love had always been with me; I was the only woman that his soul loved, and not his senses. . . . It is ever the same: stretch out your hands for life, and Death will come to you!".

"And what did you do?"

"In the first moments I did not understand

all. He again and again said he loved me a hundred times more than ever before; I was the only woman, so pure, so ideal . . . and I could not make out what he meant. But my hands, when touched by his lips, grew cold as ice.

"He was frightened, and tried to soothe me; said he would never do it any more; it was not properly his fault, he had been over-taken with wine: and besides, she—she was indeed most beautiful.

"At the bare memory, I saw his eyes flash bright. Oh, he is a *connoisseur* in women!

"And then, at last, I understood it all; and I thought (believe me, with the utmost sincerity): 'Why, rather than this, has he not been drowned in the depths of the sea?'

"A mist came before my eyes: I rubbed them to see clear. Then a sudden pain clutched at my heart and made me writhe with torture. I fainted; when I came to, I was seized with fits of hysteria. In short, I made all the scenes that the typical 'injured wife' is wont to make.

"Then, at the time when George came, I was dangerously ill. Witold did not admit that he had done me wrong, nor did he come

near me all the time.   Later, he justified himself by saying that he could have been of no
use, and was himself far too sensitive to bear
the sight of suffering.

"Finally, when all danger was over, and
Orcio was making the house ring with the
noise he made, there was the same night over
again; and he was again 'a little flushed with
wine,' and 'guilty of no offense'; again I was
'his only love.'   And later, the same scene
was repeated over and over, and at shorter
intervals.   And this day . . . it is just as
usual. . . .

"And now I am looking into the very bottom of my soul.   Have you ever seen it?   An
open coffin, in which there are no worms,
there is no corruption.   Only patches of
colour, continually fading and changing and
reviving, and forming lovely, lovely stars—
just as in a kaleidoscope.   And these hues
glisten like the scales of a serpent which rolls
and coils itself in ecstasy."

A smile passed over her face.   Then she
gave a long shudder and closed her eyes fast.

Starting up on a sudden, she joined her
hands behind her bare and shapely neck.

"If you knew, Janka," she whispered, "if

you only knew how I love him! If you knew how I am longing for him every moment when he is away! If you knew how fondly, how wildly, how madly I love the exceeding sweetness of his mouth!"

Madame Wildenhoff does not belong to the class of women that Martha was speaking of. I think that, were it not for her intrigue with Imszanski, even Martha herself might acknowledge her as a "complete woman." One may, however, be a complete woman, and yet not a complete human being. We are not yet in the habit of distinguishing these two ideas, as we distinguish between "human being" and "man." The part of a human being is one so seldom played by a woman—they have so few opportunities of doing so—that *we expect their womanliness to comprise the whole of humanity.* Nor do we realize how much we lower woman by such an expectation.

Now, as a woman, Madame Wildenhoff is complete, although her human nature cannot be said to be rich.

Her life, which she told me with the utmost frankness, has not been wanting in colour.

The daughter of a rich land-owner, she was
not yet sixteen when she crossed the frontier
to elope with a neighbour over forty, and
with whom she was not even in love! The
whole affair came about quite by chance.
She was the friend of his daughter, whom
(though he was not in favour of religious edu-
cation for women) he had decided to send to
a convent in France: and the parents of Lola
had asked him, since the two girls had made
their studies together from the very beginning, to take their daughter with him as well.
This man, having put his own daughter into
the care of the nuns, asked Lola whether, instead of poring over books in a convent, she
would not like to go with him to Italy. She
very readily agreed to what she considered
as a most natural plan. After a few months
had elapsed, she threw him over for a very
handsome Italian, who afterwards turned out
to be a Parisian Jew. After a good many
other such experiences, her parents, as a last
resort, took legal measures to find her. This
time they actually placed her in a convent:
and there, during three years of penance, her
outlook upon life took definite shape.

Her father at length relented, and allowed

her to return home, for the family had given up country life altogether, and now resided in town. There, before the year was out, she entered the married state.

Her first lover was Wartoslawski, who died some time ago; Gina Wartoslawska, whom I have mentioned, is his daughter.

No long period elapsed ere Madame Wildenhoff became unfaithful to her husband: but he, from the height of his silent scepticism, looks down with scornful amenity upon her "flirtation." It may even be that he does not dislike this state of things.

One child, a daughter, has been born of the marriage. She is two years older than Orcio; and Madame Wildenhoff has for her the greatest care and the tenderest maternal love.

I went to call upon her to-day, in the place of Martha, who is constantly unwell. She was by herself; for Wildenhoff, of course, like all husbands of his kind, either was no longer at home, or had not yet come back.

She tried to interest me by talking, as her custom is, about herself.

"My outward appearance, when all is said in its favour that can be said, is insufficient

to explain the extraordinary success I have all
my life had with men. My only ability—call
it an art if you like—consists in influencing
men by an appeal to their lower natures.
That is the only way to succeed with them:
for all of them are mere animals—all!"

She offered me some fruit, taking up the
vase containing it with the gesture of a
"hetaira" of old days, presenting a goblet of
golden wine.

"You see," she said, "I am an epicure. I
want to get as much as I can out of life, and
I know how to get it. With nothing but
champagne and songs and flowers life would
pall upon me very soon; so I like now and
then to get the atmosphere of an 'At Home':
for instance, with the Imszanskis. As to her,
I don't know whether she is really purer than
the atmosphere of a private supper-room: at
all events, her style of corruption is peculiar
—more Gothic—and the virus is more skilfully inoculated. I like to take a rest, and
spend some quiet evenings in my family circle, teach little Sophy her alphabet, or pass
sleepless nights in penance and vigil and sombre meditations. After which, I may per-
form a sudden 'pirouette', Paris style, and

blow from afar a farewell kiss to husband, Sophy, mamma, grandmamma—and virtue!"

She laughed merrily.

"The future of the nations is not what I am looking forward to. No, I am resolved to get for myself the greatest possible amount of happiness, under the circumstances in which I am placed. . . . You will say I am a mere product of environment; well, let it be so. But mind: the way I live harms no one. If I am contented, so is my husband, and so are my admirers as well."

"And their wives too?" I hazarded.

"Well, but is it my fault if they are fools? Now, I'll tell you what. Never have I taken a man from a woman he loved. I am not of those whose sole aim is to make difficult conquests."

She added, after a pause:

"For ever so long (and that you must surely know) Imszanski has been quite indifferent to his wife."

Just then the bell rang in the antechamber. Madame Wildenhoff gave a start, then burst into a fit of laughter. In that laugh of hers, I find something peculiarly interesting; but I cannot guess what.

I rose to bid her farewell.

"Why, what are you running away for? It is only Gina. I like to see two clever, handsome women together; a thing which, I must tell you, very seldom happens."

Gina came in with her customary smileless greeting, and as usual called for a glass of water. Then she set to look through certain albums, scattered about the table. Her figure, perfectly faultless in style, stood out like a sort of anachronism on the background of that florid middle-class drawing-room. In the light one could see that her eyebrows and lashes were golden, and her wavy hair of a dark auburn hue, falling in a dishevelled mass on to her shoulders as she bent forward.

Madame Wildenhoff attempted to lead the conversation towards topics of general interest.

She began by the rights of women, and their failure to understand what emancipation really signifies. Gina speaks little, but belongs, like Madame Wildenhoff, to the category of those that are emancipated in every sense of the word. As a matter of fact, her intended husband is her paramour, and

she has not the slightest intention ever to become his wife.

I have for some time noticed that she is possessed with a spirit of contradiction. In presence of people who have some certain definite
convictions, she always takes the opposite
side: this possibly in order to produce a more
striking effect by the sharp contrast of tones.
This attitude called up in my mind certain
reminiscences from out of atavistic past. I
began to talk about the gradual extinction of
individual monogamistic women, of the eroticism which has soaked our democracies
through and through, of the necessity for a
class of courtesans, that the type of those
women who care for something besides love
intrigues may be preserved, and other nonsense of similar nature.

Gina only looked at me with a drowsy
smile; but Madame Wildenhoff took up the
cudgels with a sort of enthusiasm. A curious
thing: her talk is not unlike Martha's, though
their natures are very far asunder indeed.

"Men are endowed by nature with a sense
of equilibrium: so long as they are in the
prime of life, they live and love and laugh at
plain and virtuous women. *Car il faut que*

jeunesse se passe. They therefore require what may be called the 'brute-woman'; a woman who laughs and glitters and shines for a few years, till she ages: then of course she withdraws from the arena, regretting that 'she ever followed such a path.' It is only after men have sown their wild oats that the animal dies out of them, and there wakes up— a plebeian, or a thinker, or a father, or a citizen; and then he stretches out his hands towards what we may call the 'human woman.' Then comes the triumph of her who respects herself; her day of victory has dawned, she is at last 'appreciated,' which is to say remunerated for her virtue with that famous respect which is never given to those of the other class. True, the intellectuals may complain sometimes that men will not acknowledge them as mentally their equals; but the foolish ones will be honoured by their husbands' friendship and confidence; and the good mothers will have no aim or happiness in life beyond the bringing up of children: while they each and all either look down upon the 'brute-woman' or regard them with philanthropic compassion."

"Poor things!" Gina exclaimed; "they do

not know that the tragic excitement of a single night may be perhaps worth more than a whole existence passed in such torpid apathy as theirs."

To-day there is some festival or other. I have not gone to the office, and have been sitting all the morning at Martha's bedside, who is not to get up until the afternoon. She is as usual always complaining, her sad eyes gazing into mine.

"Janka, I can no longer sleep a wink. Last night it was twelve before I ceased tossing on my pillow. Like a child, I cried myself to sleep at last: and when I woke, it was no later than three o'clock."

She crossed behind her head her lace-decked arms, and looked out into space with infinite wistfulness.

Then she continued in a low voice: "I cannot imagine why my former life in Klosow now comes back to me so very vividly. I remember how sometimes I used to rise early on a winter morning, when it was still dark, and how I dressed by lamplight, shivering with cold, and fighting down my longing to go back to my warm bed. Then I would put on a huge fur, and take the keys, and go to the farm with a lantern in my hand. Do you know, all this is present to me now, just like a vision? And then I remember the far-off fields, lying fallow beneath the snow, and stretching away even to the verge of the horizon, under the sky in which the stars were beginning to grow pale. I remember the farm buildings, vague dark spots upon the landscape, the forests like streaks of violet, the grey fences, and the delicate tracery of the leafless garden trees. And now through the darkness there come sounds: the clattering of tin pails, and the faint drowsy calling of the maids to one another. Oh, and I remember well the cold, the lusty, fresh, piercing cold, making the teeth clatter in one's head. And then, the close warmth of the cow-byres, and the low black-raftered ceiling overhead; the outlines of the solemn-looking cows and sleepy milkmaids, the bright circles of the lanterns on the floor, and the quaint broken shadows on the beams and girders above; the milk stream rhythmically into the pails, the indolent lowing of the kine, and the jingling sound of the chain that bound the savage steer to the crib. . . . You remember the cat,

too—our cat? Don't you: so sharp of wit,
following us everywhere like a dog? All
that's so far off, so irrevocably gone! Oh, I
tell you, I would give more than my life, if I
could but see one such morning return—only
one such bleak and dark and frosty morning,
and I were now as I was then! . . ."

She turned her cheek to the pillow, and
shed tears.

"Martha, your nerves are again in a very
poor state. If you like, I shall go with you
to Klosow; and we shall spend Christmas
there together, and enjoy a few idyllic days
as of old."

"Oh, no, Janka; they would only be the miserable ghosts of times that are past for ever.
That stupid, clubby-faced woman, Janusz's
wife, would get on my nerves so; besides, the
thought that Witold would be staying here
with Madame Wildenhoff, and glad I was
away!

"But," she added with a sudden revival of
spirits, "do you know, I fancy her triumph
will be over pretty soon? It is true that
Witold was never very much attached to her:
but now it would seem that his affections are
strongly engaged elsewhere."

"Are they?" I asked, much interested: for I recalled Lipka and my unexpected meeting with Imszanski there.

"Did he tell you anything?"

"Oh, he is simply ridiculous—so hopelessly frank with me. He never will spare me any details, and holds it in some sort as a duty to conceal nothing from me. . . ."

She laughed bitterly, and at once looked sullen again.

"Yesterday, before you came home from the office, I asked Witold all about her. She is some star of the Parisian *demi-monde*, who has made up her mind to get an engagement at any price on the stage here: and Witold is expected, on account of his influence in Warsaw, to obtain a fixed situation for her. It appears that her voice is tolerable, and her outward appearance marvellous: he has described her to me in every particular. It was, I assure you, one of the most emotional experiences I ever went through."

She closed her eyes, to intensify the image that she was forming in her mind.

"The woman is tall, and seemingly of spare proportions: but only seemingly so. Her bony framework is exceedingly slight and

reed-like: so you see, Janka, on close inquiry
she is found not to be really thin."

As she spoke, she turned upon her pillow,
tearing at its satin covering with her nails, and
striving to swallow down her tears of rage.

I could not contain myself.

"Why on earth does he tell you about such
things? He must be a monster."

"There are a great many things that he
never can understand—what I told you seems
but the merest trifle to him."

She took a spoonful of bromide, and continued:

"You must know that he tells me she has
large oval-shaped eyes, with extremely long
lashes—eyes of an unfathomable black, in
very striking contrast with her voluptuous
mouth; always sorrowful, dreamy, and with
a far-away look, like the beggar-maid loved
by King Cophetua. She has also much
originality, something like an odalisque, and
uniting the primitiveness of a mountain goat
with all the cultured grace of a maid of
honour at a royal court."

This, after the elimination of certain exaggerated points, was easily recognizable as
the description of that fair French-woman

whom I had seen at Lipka's. And now I understood why Imszanski had shown himself so very full of courtesy toward Czolhanski. The latter, as a theatrical critic, may be useful to him.

"She dresses, it appears, most superbly, with all the magnificence of Babylonian times: golden combs and strings of pearls in her hair; in her ears, rings of the greatest price. Moreover, she is a very miracle of depravity. Witold smiled as he told me so, with an inward look, as though recalling some particular.

"As he told me so, he smiled; and I too smiled, listening with the blandest interest. He looked at me attentively, kissed my hand, and said:

" 'Your nerves are better now, I see. How glad I am! You have no idea. You have at last realized that to feel jealous of a *cocotte* would be unworthy of you.'

" 'Why, of course. Yes, yes; I am all right now.' And yet, Janka, I never felt it so deeply; I never saw things with such awful clearness of vision. And alas! I never, never yet loved Witold with such passionate love.

"But, more than him, I love that pain which I feel. . . ."

She rose in bed, as if to repel something that was weighing her down; then she sat propped up by her cushions and pillows.

"Do you imagine that in all this I had any idea of revengeful pleasure at Mme. Wildenhoff's disappointment, and for that reason made him tell me what he did? Not in the least. I wanted to drink my fill of pain; as in Spain they wave a red flag in bull-fights before the bloodshot eyes of the poor brute, to make him yet madder with rage and despair, so I wished to excite myself to the same delirious state.

"I do not wish for anything that can diminish the intensity of my anguish, I hate whatever could mitigate or deaden it. I love to gloat over the raw bleeding wounds, bare and unbandaged. . . ."

At that moment, the nurse tapped at the door, to ask whether Orcio might not come in to bid his mother good morning.

"No—no! shut the door! I will have no one here! Janka, you have not the least idea how I *hate* my son."

At Lipka's to-night: and this time in a private room. Mme. Wildenhoff talked at great length, somewhat to the following effect:

"There is in reality only one kind of perfect love—that of the brute creation; indeliberate, irreflective love, wherein victory is to the strongest and most beautiful; the pure reproductive instinct, unalloyed by any culture or mental analysis whatsoever. But we—we, who are civilized—unfortunately look down upon this sort of love. For we have reckoned, with quasi-mathematical exactitude, how much of love should be taken, and how much rejected, in order to get the greatest possible sum of quintessential delight. And thence has sprung quite a new type of love: instinct which has emancipated itself from obedience to the laws of nature—love with its chief motive, preservation of the species, eliminated. Now love of the kind I have spoken of generally receives the epithet of bestial; whereas on the contrary it is most specially the outcome of refinement."

"It appears among nations at the epoch of their highest development, and is the harbinger of their speedy decline," remarked Czolhanski, with solemn dignity.

"What does it matter? *Après nous le
déluge!*"

"And to what class would you assign con-
jugal love?" asked Owinski. Gina, who had
silently disposed her lithe, snake-like, supple
figure on a little sofa, looked round with astonishment at her *fiancé*.

"Oh, we may call it love of a third type,"
answered Madame Wildenhoff: "love sanc-
tioned by law, the union of two souls in friendship, and the bringing forth of rachitic offspring: an abnormal combination of brute
and human love."

"Do you then, Madame," urged Owinski,
"perceive no good points in marriage?"

"None whatever," she replied with a bland
smile, "because—and this reason alone would
suffice me—because I hate marriage with all
my heart. It has been and is the aim of my
life to blast marriage, whenever I can succeed in doing so. Between the happiest and
most moral couples—those in which one of
the two, the husband or the wife, leads a prof-
ligate life, and the other knows nothing of it
—I bring the dissolving element, enlightenment, and rejoice when I see the couples fall
apart."

Here she bent aside toward her husband's chair, and said to him in an affectionate and audible whisper:

"But we are a pattern couple, are we not?"

This time, Imszanski went home with me. I overheard Czolhanski say, on taking leave of him: "You may rely upon me absolutely; I will manage everything."

It has been terribly cold, and now there is a thaw. At such times, I love to wander up and down the avenues in the park, which then are completely deserted.

My nostrils inhale that peculiar scent of bare moist earth, and the effluvium from the buds as yet invisible; and I muse upon those incomparable and marvellously beautiful things that have never been realized.

On the yellow background of dry dead grass, there appeared in the distance a young man to whom, as to myself, loneliness was no doubt pleasant, and who enjoyed walking along the avenues oversprinkled with last year's fallen leaves.

He came up with me, and on passing by, looked keenly into my eyes, and with something of astonishment.

I did not return his glance, but walked
more slowly, so as to lag behind him.

The young man stopped presently, and
waited until I came up; then he passed by me
again with a protracted stare.

This manœuvre was repeated several times.
Presently I was seized with an unaccountable
desire to burst into a fit of nervous laughter,
which I smothered down as best I could. At
any rate, I had the full control of my eyes,
the expression of which was mere indifference
and disdain. Presently I looked him stead-
ily in the face, to stare him out of countenance; so that he could see my attitude to be
unmistakably hostile.

"But why," I was thinking all the time,
"why should I look upon him—this handsome slender stripling—as my foe? He certainly does not mean to harm me in any way;
his interest is simply aroused in finding a person who has the same taste for solitude as himself, whilst he naturally has a friendly feeling
towards a good-looking woman."

The young fellow, at first kindly disposed,
was nettled by the look of hostility in my
eyes. He came up close to me, with a flippant

laugh, and said in an ironical tone of sympathy:

"I would give anything in reason to know what sorrows of the heart have driven you to take so very romantic a walk as this."

I was silent, and knit my brows.

"Souls that pine in loneliness," he went on, as sarcastic as before, "ought to comfort each other, I think: don't you?"

There was a pause, as we walked side by side.

"But why knit those fair eyebrows so? Oh, really, you frighten me. . . . Such malignant eyes! Come, come, I shall do you no harm; why be so cantankerous?"

In a rage and turning my back on him, I walked swiftly away. He made no attempt to follow. On arriving at the gate, where I was safe at last, I looked round. He was standing where he had stood before, and from afar waving me with bared head a graceful farewell.

The incident mortified and abashed me. I had behaved like a silly goose, narrow-minded and ill-tempered; I had spoiled a situation that might have had pleasant or curious developments. Why on earth had I done so?

Was this, again, only a matter of form? The necessity of that regular introduction, so dear to the *bourgeoisie,* in a drawing-room where two persons are made acquainted with each other by a third? Or was it not rather that dread—now a part of our life—the instinctive dread of things as they are, the eternal need of playing the part of a besieged fort, which defends itself stubbornly in order to surrender on the best terms possible?

As I came out of the park, a carriage driven at full speed passed by me; I saw a couple of feathers and a good deal of fur. Suddenly the coachman pulled up, and Mme. Wildenhoff jumped out and came towards me.

"Ah! how delighted I am to meet you! You won't get away from me this time. Pray step in: I must make a regular woman of you."

"With pleasure: but what's the matter?"

"You shall hear."

We got in. Mme. Wildenhoff gave the man orders to drive slowly.

"Quite a warm day!" she observed. . . .

"Well, you see, I have one *idée fixe,* at least that's what my husband calls it."

"And that is? . . ."

"Ah, what a coincidence to have met you, of whom I was just thinking!"

"Very good, but what do you want me for?"

"Wait a bit; I must begin at the beginning.

"Let me tell you that I consider it a most important point that we should, in the cause of Woman, meet and come to an understanding with women of so-called 'loose character.' And, in particular, enter into social relations with them. It is indeed an eccentricity on my part; but I enjoy stemming and making head against the current."

"It may lead to curious developments," I said.

"You are perfectly right. In the first place, we must all of us get to understand our community of interests. The social boycott which the whole *demi-monde* has to undergo, is a real civil war waged by women against one another; a weakening of our powers, to which men not only do not object, but which they also tend to aggravate. It is they who make 'those dreadful creatures, bereft of a conscience,' responsible for all the transgressions

which they themselves commit: so that the
fury of jealousy which their mothers and
their wives, actual or intended, would otherwise pour out upon their heads, is all transformed into a feeling of hatred against such
women. It is undoubtedly a very clever bit
of tactics on their part; but we ought not to
let ourselves be taken in so easily; we should
all close our ranks and join shoulder to shoulder to fight the common foe."

"But what if those women hate us more
than we do them?"

"That they do, is true; but it is only because they believe us to be happier than they
are. We have to dispel this egregious delusion; we must let them know that we feel
our wrongs as keenly as they do theirs; that
we recognize them as our companions in
womanhood, as sharers in our common humanity. . . . It is because we do nothing that
such a falsehood has been able to take such
strong root.

"We should join with them, for they are
our necessary complement: not only so, but
mingle with them without endeavouring to intensify the difference between us and them by
trying, in so far as we can, to deprive our

souls of those immense fields of womanliness, and renounce to our own detriment the glamour of frivolity and of frailty. There must be a thorough fusion; and it is only by such levelling down that we shall arrive at the synthesis of womanhood: a new type, a complete type, in which the only difference observable will be those of individuals, not of avocations."

"All that's very fine, but where are you taking me?"

"I am coming to that. I am just paying a formal visit to an ex-courtesan, a Mme. Wieloleska—formerly Mary *tout court,* for I don't know her family name. And I absolutely want you to come along with me."

"But . . . is she possible?"

"Quite; you may believe me. She takes everything as a matter of course, and will be much pleased to receive you. . . . Only you will have to behave exactly as if she were Wieloleski's real wife."

"What? then they are not married?"

"The idea! The man has a wife and five children somewhere down in the country. . . . And that woman has got such a hold on him that he won't stir so much as one step from her side. . . . You must take a look at their place. . . . She was formerly quite a common *demi-mondaine,* though well spoken of."

"And how did you get to know her?"

"Oh, she's an old acquaintance, made by means of Imszanski."

The carriage had stopped in front of an ornamental gateway, leading to a handsome suburban villa, screened from view to some extent by a tracery of branches and tree-trunks, and in a frame of towering fir-trees.

As I went up the broad white steps at the entrance, I felt my heart beat, and could not tell exactly why. Perhaps at the fancy which then came to me, that I might, within those very doors, come face to face with the naked, dark, and horrible mystery of Life!

An elderly and very stylish footman raised the door-hanging to usher us into a large sitting-room, conventionally furnished *à la sécession.*

In a few minutes there entered a very tall, slim, lady-like person, quietly dressed in a clinging morning gown, somewhat like a riding-habit, and followed by a little white lamb,

which came treading stiffly and sometimes
funnily sliding along the polished floor.

Mme. Mary welcomed Mme. Wildenhoff
with smiling effusion.

"I have come to call upon you with a friend
of mine: Miss Dernowicz, Mme. Wieloleska," she said, introducing me. "I trust you
will have no objection; I wanted to show her
your greenhouse very much."

"Indeed, my dear Madame, but you are
doing me a pleasure. I feel so bored in this
solitude, where I see nobody at all. All day
long, my husband is in the greenhouse or pot-
tering about the hotbeds; he has engaged a
new gardener from Haarlem, and it is quite
out of the question getting him anywhere out
of doors. If you care, we shall have a look
at the greenhouse at once. I tell you, if it
were not for my books and studies, I really
might be tempted to make away with myself."

"And why should you not take a walk sometimes? The weather is splendid just now."

"Oh, no! My husband won't go out; and it
would not be proper for a woman to go out
alone. You know how uncharitable people
are."

"And what may you be studying, Madame?" I asked.

"Pretty nearly everything possible," she replied, laughing. "I take at least five hours of lessons daily. One of my professors only just left the house: he is giving me a course of University lessons on the ancient literature of India. Since a week, too, I have been learning to read hieroglyphics. . . . Haven't you made a study of them? . . . They are very interesting. . . . One is carried away— other lands, other times. . . . And I am so curious about everything in the world. . . . But I am best in languages. It is so extremely important to be able to read every writer in the original."

"For you must know," put in Mme. Wildenhoff, "that Mme. Mary is a well-known linguist."

"Indeed?"

"Ah," she said, smiling modestly, "it all comes to me so easily. At the present time, I am proficient in French, English, German, Italian, Spanish, Swedish, Dutch, and Russian. This year I am learning the Finnish and Japanese languages. I have, moreover, read Homer and Virgil in the original Greek and Latin. Not one hundredth part of their marvellous beauties can be rendered in a translation: and I am so sensitive to the Beautiful . . . !"

"Do you know?" she broke off, turning towards Mme. Wildenhoff, "I have at last managed to satisfy my husband that we must positively take a trip to Algeria. And that will have to be in a few weeks: it is too hot there in summer. . . . Ah! you can't think how hard it is to get him away from those flowers of his; he loves them so dearly!"

I examined Mme. Wieloleska with careful scrutiny. Her face is pale and surrounded with scanty locks of fair hair; her eyes, small, greyish and expressionless, and bordered with a faint pink hue, are continually in motion to and fro; she has a tiny nose with rounded nostrils, and a full, rather bloodless mouth, now and then moving with a quick twitch, like a child making a wry face; and with all that she is attractive. Her talkativeness, her tuneless voice, and a certain carelessness in her manner, correct one's first impression that she is pretentious, and give the effect of a schoolgirl *désinvolture,* rather than the effrontery of a *bona-roba.*

She stooped to caress her pet lamb, which had lain down at her feet in a posture that suggested careful training. Then she rose, saying: "Perhaps we may now go and look at the place."

On our way to the conservatory, we had to pass through several rooms and galleries full of pictures. On the right, we saw a workroom, with bright jets of gas burning, though the night had not yet fallen. Several girls were there, busily bending over tambour frames.

"These are my little ones," said Mme. Wieloleska, smiling at them. "Unfortunately, I have no children myself, so I have undertaken to bring up these girls."

"What are they about here?"

"They are learning embroidery, under the tuition of a German instructress. I am particularly anxious that my philanthropic plans may not do them more harm than good; for my husband very wisely says that 'it is not hard to give, but to give judiciously. . . .'"

"Well, but what do you do with the embroidered work afterwards?"

"Oh, you see, I don't like to wear lace upon my linen—besides, it is not the fashion now-a-days—so I have everything covered over with embroidery. Linen is far more beautiful so. I—I might perhaps show you—yes, I think it's all right here—only women present. . . ."

She laughed, winking significantly, and took us farther down the passage, where, with a swift twist and twirl, like a ballet-dancer, she raised her dress above her knees, showing several tiers of cambric flounces beyond her silk stockings. At no other time of our visit was there anything to recall what she had once been.

"You, I fancy," she said, turning to me, "wear a petticoat; I am not sure you had not better give it up. A well-flounced undergarment makes the dress look quite sufficiently wide; a petticoat altogether effaces the outlines of the hips." Then passing her hand down my waist: "It is a pity," she said; "for you have a splendid shape—hips like a Spanish woman's."

We have found Wieloleski standing at the very end of the conservatory, and carefully watching his gardener at work. He is a tall man, something over forty, rather stout; very elegant-mannered, and courteous, but distant and abstracted. He has an extensive bald place, with long thin wisps combed over it from the left, though without any attempt at concealment; and an abundant black beard.

As he was taking us about his greenhouse, he observed: "It is only at present, and since I have been living here, that I have learned to understand Tolstoi properly. It is only by a close acquaintance with nature and with manual work, that we discover all the emptiness of society life and its form and prejudices, and all the futility of social dissensions and hatreds."

I am not so well able to maintain my position as a cool observer, as Mme. Wildenhoff is: and here I could not refrain from presenting an objection to him.

"And nevertheless, your being able to stand thus aside in social struggles, proceeds from the fact that you possess property; and property itself lies within the sphere of these struggles, since they make an object of it. So the very land you own brings you back into these classes of society from which you flee."

Wieloleski, rather surprised, offered me a few white kalia flowers, just gathered, before he replied, in a calm but very dogmatic tone.

"On this point, I cannot agree with you.

Those who dispute the right of property take no account of the reality of things. Immemorial custom has made the right of property as much a 'category of thought,' as Space is, or Time."

Mary, who was just behind us, interrupted him: "Oh, Edmund is reading you a lecture already, I hear. My dear, you had better come and flirt with Mme. Lola, and I'll take Miss Janina with me."

She came and put her arm round my waist, saying that she liked me very much indeed. This I answered with an indulgent smile, always suitable when women pay compliments to women.

She felt that this was not the way to win me, so she set to talk about literature.

"There are some books," she said, "in which I find a rest, and which enable me to escape from reality altogether. And that's why I can't bear such authors—Zola, for instance— as bring dirt which ought to revolt any delicate mind, into a sphere where poetry alone should reign supreme."

I hazarded another objection here.

"Do you not think that the first step

towards healing the ulcers of society is to lay
them bare?"

"Ugh! why write about them? We all
know them too well! In life itself, there is,
I tell you, quite enough of sorrow and of
miasma. You, so young, may possibly not
have as yet had any opportunity of coming
into contact with them. . . . No, no: why
should we ourselves spoil the short sweet
moments when it is possible to dream?"

She then proposed that we should take a
rest on a seat of bamboo-work, ensconced
amongst exotic plants and shrubs in large
green tubs. As soon as we had sat down, her
trained pet lamb came and lay down on the
skirt of her dress.

"Every one ought to have some sacred book
—some Bible or other—ought he not?" she
asked, after a short silence. "Alas! there is
no one, with ever so little knowledge of philosophy, who can possibly believe in the existence of God—and all the rest of it.

"But we can at any rate respect the poetry
which religion contains, and the feelings of
those who have not as yet lost their faith: is
it not so?"

"Certainly," I replied with the utmost gravity.

"Well, the Bible which I could not go to sleep without reading, and out of which I read portions daily instead of my prayers, is that book of legends by Voragine. . . . Do you know it?"

"Oh, yes," I assented, "the *Golden Legend.*"

"Oh, what a world of poetry there is in it! What treasures of freshness and simplicity of feeling!"

"Well, I say! if they are all of her kidney!" was all I remarked to Mme. Wildenhoff, as I returned with her after our half-hour's call at Wieloleski's. I felt a good deal bored, and mused over the meaning of the well-known aphorism:

Dans la bête assouvie un ange se réveille.[1]

For some time Imszanski has been spending his evenings at home! He either goes out later in the evening, or not at all, and Martha's hopes are reviving within her; but I do not take this conversion of his very seriously.

We three sit together frequently; now and

When the brute's gorged, an angel wakes within it.

then Czolhanski and Owinski, or Rosuchow-
ski drop in.

One peculiarity about Owinski is the continual vague absent look in his eyes, caused
by his extremely short sight. He cannot see
two paces in front of him, and distinguishes
people by their voices only. His facial mus-
cles are in constant play; and he never smiles
but with set teeth. He is very far indeed
from being good-looking; yet I do not wonder at Gina's loving him to distraction.

Witold has been pleased to take me as his
confidante now. He is probably feeling com-
punction for his recent behaviour, somewhat
late in the day.

Life, taken in general, is a barren waste.
His theory of love does not permit him to
hold innocent those delusions of the senses
which are usually termed "bits of love-making," though in reality, they and love have
nothing in common. They are then evil; but
they have become necessary evils, to which
men have in the course of ages completely
accustomed themselves; evils from which
women—he means of course those of the better classes—are free, and against which they
ought to be guarded with the utmost care.

By means of this reasoning, he considers his relations with Martha to be all they should be; for he always endeavoured to spare her, and to preserve her high ideals, and her feelings of purity.

I could not help smiling as he said this, knowing as I did how little his intention had been realized.

But now he too seems to be tiring of the life he leads—this howling wilderness of a life. "These women are so shallow, so mindless, so fatuous! Their own looseness of morals is the key-note which decides every one of their acts."

I could now shrewdly guess what his drift was.

"Take, for instance, Mme. Wildenhoff. She enjoys a change of—affections—once a month. That's her business: but why the devil does she bring in Philosophy and Sociology, and Emancipation? The thing she does is as old as the hills, and why trouble about her and women like her?"

I had long ago made the remark that men object to women who argue. On the other hand, they rate their souls very high indeed. Now, Witold confesses, it is the soul—the soul alone, the soul at any price—that he wants to have.

Who knows whether he will not again become a faithful husband to Martha?

I dislike all colourless people. And I dislike myself along with them, since I find I am growing more and more colourless day by day. I feel out of sympathy with my own type of character: I am ordinary. I have had enough of my life; more than enough of it.

How terribly I am craving now for some one who shall tell me—and tell me incessantly—that I am good-looking and clever and original in mind, that I dress nicely and move gracefully.

For though at this moment I am quite satisfied that none of these things are so: yet, if I were told so this day, I should at once believe it to be true.

I am in pain. At times I feel a special need of saying all that I think. At times it is so hard to wear a mask. . . . And I want some sympathy. . . .

I was at the Wildenhoff's to-day, and had a talk with Witold. I cannot conceive how it came about, but on a sudden I found I was saying too much—or rather, speaking too much to the point.

Finding the position I had taken up was too advanced and too much exposed, I decided to beat a retreat.

"But can you conceive in what the tragedy of my life consists in reality?" I asked.

On which, in mute questioning, he raised his beautiful mournful eyes to mine.

"In that all I have told you is untrue . . . and all I have not told you is untrue likewise. It is my style to talk of my sadness one day, and the next to tell of my life's cloudless philosophy."

"And to whom of all men do you tell the truth? To Wiazewski? I don't know. Perhaps to no one. When I have taken off, one after another, all the styles I wear, there is nothing more left of me."

At this juncture, Mme. Wildenhoff, dressed in a very low-cut black velvet gown, came up to us.

"Why has not Martha been here to-day?" she asked. "We have not seen her for ever so long."

"She meant to come but she is continually a victim to sick headaches."

"Ah, yes, those sick headaches," she remarked sympathizingly. "They are so very hard to get rid of!"

Presently she asked if I would come and look at a beautiful screen, a birthday gift for her, painted by Gina. Imszanski remained where he was.

I asked Mme. Wildenhoff why Owinski was not present.

"Really, I cannot say," was her answer. "He was to come: but it is rather late."

"I noticed that Gina was very much out of sorts to-day."

"Yes, and I must say that I feel rather uneasy about her. There is something here that I cannot at all understand, and I love the girl. . . . Owinski is perpetually wool-gathering; he is a man you cannot rely upon. . . . He strikes me as one who would be deaf to any remonstrances, any reproaches. . . . He is a typical poet. . . ."

"Then it may be that Gina is wrong in holding off from marriage with the man."

"Marriage? A fine thing that would be! She is surely wealthy enough to do without it. . . . Marriage!" she added, not without a touch of pride. "Of what use was it in Imszanski's case, I beg?"

She just looked into a mirror, hanging opposite her bed, and then swiftly glanced over me from head to foot. The comparison between us must have been not unpleasant, for she at once became more cheerful and friendly.

"My dear Miss Janina, Gina's is a nature far too artistic for marriage. No one who can paint like that would ever make a husband of her sweetheart. Pardon me; the thing is absolutely out of the question. . . . Look at those flowers; with what grace she has dashed them off!"

"They are certainly exquisite. But did you notice how extraordinary an interest Owinski took in what you were saying about marriage last Thursday?"

"Yes, oh, yes; I remember. . . . But I can't suppose he is thinking of marrying any one else. . . . No, that is surely impossible."

She was at once in a state of great excitement.

"Look here. Now that marriage is no more than a contract, assuring to the wife board and lodging for self and offspring, and to the husband a woman in permanency, always at home and on the *qui vive;* now that a bachelor cannot marry until he has achieved a position in the world, so that a marrying man who is not bald sounds like a *contradictio in adjecto,*—marriage amounts in principle to the same as prostitution, whereas its every particular is yet more shocking."

"I am afraid I don't quite follow you."

"Why, the thing is as clear as clear can be. A courtesan makes only a temporary bargain, and if she makes it for a longer time, she always reserves to herself complete liberty of action, some intervals of freedom, and the power of breaking her chain whenever she pleases; whilst the 'honest woman' makes the bargain for her whole life, without any hope of ever being set free: for we need not take divorce into account, were it but for the fact that a divorced woman is adversely viewed by her 'honest' sisters. . . . A common courtesan, even one who lodges in a house of ill fame, has her 'Alphonse,' some one to whom, and some place wherein she can give sincere, true and disinterested love, which the average honest woman cannot dare to allow herself, without the imminent danger of losing her right of alimony. Now, as to the moral difference. It lies in this: that one possesses only one husband, together with the respect of society, whereas the other has many, and is despised. Though I cannot for the life of me see what logical connection there is between a number of lovers and the obligation for a woman to respect the rights of humanity. Again: the police take charge of the street-walker's health; but who sees after the wife that her own husband has contaminated? The former may die of *anything;* the other, the honest woman, in childbed, if married; if not—if, having no portion, she cannot have a husband—she may die of what you will—and there you are! And Abolitionists arrange congresses, publish books and pamphlets, found philanthropic institutions, refuges, Christian associations to raise fallen women, and young people's leagues to shield their purity during school-years. All this, to what purpose? That a common doctor, and not the police, should see after the street-girl's health; that a few silly females should be shut up, not in bagnios, but in sewing-rooms; and that some women may have to teach their husbands certain things which the latter have not yet learnt! And all this in the interest of 'coming generations!' An empty phrase. Is not all that most ridiculous?"

She laughed; but to me her words were painful.

"But then, instead of this, are we to do nothing?"

"Not at all. Let us found homes and refuges: not for the women, but for the children whose mothers are unable to take care of them. And as to the so-called ignominy, that will remain; but we ought to laugh it to scorn. And allow me to add," she went on, in a more earnest tone, "that to loosen in so far as we can all artificial bonds is a far easier and a more natural task than to draw them still tighter. Both roads lead to the same goal,—with the difference that in one case the goal would signify freedom, and in the other slavery."

As she spoke, I remembered what Witold had said to me about her.

She abruptly broke off. "Oh, let's join the company! What will they think of a hostess who neglects her guests so!"

In the drawing-room, Owinski had not

made his appearance as yet. Gina, as beautiful as a portrait by some Old Master, was reclining silently, in an amaranthine-coloured easy-chair.

Imszanski shot a glance and a faint smile at Mme. Wildenhoff, and offered me his arm to go in to supper.

Whoever it was—Amiel, I think,—who maintained that women do not care to be analyzed, was in the wrong. It is rather men who dislike such analysis.

Why does a woman rarely fall in love with a man inferior to herself? Because she wants to be loved for all that is in her. And thence proceeds the grievance, not less distasteful than groundless, that men do not look on women as having minds as well as bodies. Now a man is quite satisfied if the woman acknowledges his superiority over her.

Those whom I like best are not those who attract me most, but who are able to comprehend and to realize my whole power of attraction. That is why I dislike to hear Imszanski babbling, in a superficial and general manner, of the excellence of my nature, not knowing in what it consists, and unable to grasp it.

And that, too, is why I have a liking for

Wiazewski, and a wish that he could find it in his heart to love me.

Spring is coming. With a hot sun overhead, there is a cool breeze around. I feel joyful, and frolicsome, and full of animal spirits. I could fall upon the neck of the first man I met in the street! To be loved by somebody, that is my craving. I might feel less fearfully alone and cut off from everything in the world,—I would give many a year of my life. Lord! if anyone would kiss me . . . now!—Only, not one of those . . . Oh, not one of them!

So many years have passed away since that parting, never to fade out of my mind! Yes: he was the only man I could ever have loved. . . . How quickly it all passed away, and how completely it all came to an end! Strange.— A bit of life.

And now it sleeps, that happiness,—sleeps beneath the flowery palls of many a springtime, past and gone.

Such a spring; oh, well-a-day! And in my heart and life all is so blank and so dismal!

I have lived but a short, a very short time; and notwithstanding, how many and how fair

flowers of memory have I culled! If I could
only remember them all—all of them—why,
then, life would be endurable still.

And I am ever, as I go on, closer and closer
to life: I wade along, athwart its foaming and
tempestuous current; but it is in vain I would
try to plunge into its waves and moisten these
lips of mine, so parched with thirst,—as if I
were traversing a sea of quicksilver, whose dry
metallic drops fly into liquid dust when they
are touched.

And still I have to wait—to wait—to wait
for something else, something like the spring
in its glamour and its sunshine—to wait for a
marvel, a prodigy, a miracle, that is to come!

In company with Gina and Owinski, I was
just leaving a coffee-house. In front of us,
surrounded by several men, there walked a
woman, rather thickset, far from tall, who
wore a short-skirted, bright-coloured dress,
and a wide-brimmed hat, also of a bright hue.
She went slowly, with an undulating motion
of the hips, turning, now to right, now to left,
now behind her, chattering with lively interest, and addressing them all together, her
hands meanwhile nimble with gestures like
those of a flower-girl offering nosegays. We

caught glimpses of her profile,—very long lashes and a short straight nose. There seemed to be some witchery wafted towards me from that figure.

"A *cocotte?*" I asked Gina.

She looked at her, and nodded, with a lowering face.

We had previously been talking of love. She resumed the subject where I had interrupted her.

. . . "Ah, but I am not by any means telling you it is absolute bliss. No. Love only intensifies all things whatever: and thus, not joy only, but pain as well. Love is an exceedingly powerful stimulant, the strengthener of all that belongs to life. And this, when all its colours are thus suddenly brightened up, becomes like some magic fairy tale, some eternal Divine Vision of life. . . ."

Owinski, plunged deep in his musings, was not listening to us at all, though Gina spoke especially for him. The golden fire which flashed in her eyes died out when she realized this.

"We ourselves are alone in fault; it is we who have brought about that immense misery, the fiery pain of which is now eating our hearts out. For every time we have turned a man away from us, every denial of the lips that belied the pulsing of the blood is a sin against Life. Every such night, when those who craved love for love received it not, but were perforce obliged to purchase it with gold, is a sin against Life—of which *we* are guilty.

"And therefore should we all—like consecrated priestesses,—go forth:—forth to suffering and to shame, with the laughter of Spring, and its cry *Evoë!* love for love, joy for joy, pain for pain,—welling up from our hearts!"

"But why then pain?"

"I do not know; but so it has to be. Surely you feel that intense joy is not to be purchased without intense pain."

Owinski, looking down the long vista of the street, took not the slightest interest in what she was saying. Gina became silent; it may be that a feeling of shame had come upon her.

The strangely bewitching woman had stopped, coming to a sudden standstill to take leave of some of her companions. Her laughter resounded through the brightly lit, deserted street, with all the effrontery and witchery of Life itself.

Half-consciously, Owinski turned towards

her, and so did we; a breath of the coming spring seemed blowing in our direction thence.

"Is she to your taste?" Gina asked her fiancé, with a curiosity in her tone of voice that she strove to make light of.

"What did you say?—oh, I don't know, didn't see her," he returned. wool-gathering as usual.

Wishing to please her, he again turned round to look; but the whole company had already disappeared in the doorway of a neighbouring restaurant.

Gina took his arm, with a gesture of famished and baffled desire. Laying her head on the sleeve of his great-coat, she brushed a wisp of hair from her cheek.

"No," she said to me in an undertone; "no, I cannot tell; I myself am ignorant of the end for which suffering exists; why must there always be suffering?"

Still Owinski heard not a word we said; so we could converse quite freely. For my part, I could not love a man so continually lost in thought.

"Seldom have I happened upon a type in such sharp contrast to all that I am," she con-

tinued, alluding to the woman we had just
seen.

Far down in Gina's eyes, whose nervous energy was tired and worn out,—somewhere
very deep down,—there shone a livid gleam
of disquiet.

She gazed searchingly at her fiancé, but
there was no change in the expression of his
face. After a time, he was aware that her
glance was upon him; then he bent forward
to her, and, stroking her glove, said smiling:

"What is the matter with you, Gina?"

"Nothing—only love for you," she whispered.

Afterwards, we sat with Mme. Wildenhoff
almost till dawn.

"What's to be done? If he loves her no
longer, he cannot be forced to stay with her,"
said Mme. Lola to me, speaking of Owinski,
of course. "Changes in feeling have nothing
in common with ethics and the sense of duty."
. . . And so on, and so on.

Gina approached us presently.

"To-morrow I shall be living by myself,"
she told us. "I am now in such a state that
I can't bear any one, not even so amiable a
person as Idalia. She will live in my studio,

which she likes very much, and the room that she rented formerly will now be let. I should greatly like to find another tenant for her."

Mme. Wildenhoff turned upon me directly with these unexpected words:

"Wouldn't you like to lodge with Idalia? She plays so beautifully; and that family life must, I fancy, bore you by now."

It then occurred to me that Mme. Wildenhoff's intention was to get me away from Imszanski! Was I right? Possibly.

"I shall think it over," I answered in a pleasant tone. "Though indeed I like just as much to hear Martha play."

This staying up all night long nearly once every forty-eight hours or so fatigues me beyond measure. They—that is, all the others —have nothing to do; they rise at noon, and enjoy plenty of money and leisure; and their greatest enjoyment is talking interminably about the deepest problems of existence. But for me, what with having battle with sleep in the morning, to walk so very far to my office through mud and slush, and to sit motionless at my desk for so many hours, those nights charge me with a burden very hard to bear.

I have, it is true, a frame of iron: but such a life would wear it out at length.

I am weary and miserable, and from time to time I feel almost distracted. My state is that of one who has an appointment, and waits, waits, waits, through the hours and through the years, although the time allotted to keep it has long since passed by. I experience the same fever of impatience, the same clutching at my heart, when in my delusion I think I can at last hear his footsteps; the same chill of terror, when for an instant I think he will never come.

All this is very banal, very "missish." Yes, I know, I know. But now and then it is simply beyond my power to keep down, simply overwhelming. For the time assigned to me, the wonderful time of meeting with one whom I love, fled into the past so long, so long ago!

Ah, it has come, that time! It came yesterday. I had already felt it in the air for many a day; it was in Martha's eyes; my own heart told me. And while I yearned for it constantly, yet did I fear it like a sentence of death.

Having returned long after Martha had

fallen asleep, he noticed that there was a light in my room, and tapped gently. I did not answer: nevertheless he came in.

"How late you have stayed up reading!" he said in a whisper. And then, seating himself on the couch beside me, he remained silent.

Covering my eyes with my hands, I let my head droop as low as to his knees, and in an instant was possessed with a mad, frenzied effervescence of expectancy. I shivered all over as with the ague; then shook all over with soundless laughter. Something was leaping up in my breast, palpitating in my very throat, in my brain, in my hands that were covering my eyes. . . . Had this unparalleled excitement lasted but one moment more I should have cried out aloud with terror and agony.

Then in an instant I grew quiet, overwhelmed with a sense of sudden numbness: and I let my head droop yet lower. Witold bent over me, and kissed my hair and shoulders. And then he raised up my head, and showered kisses on my eyes and mouth and throat.

Not one word of love did we speak. Already, long before, we had understood one another. But there were a thousand thoughts rushing through my brain.

He bent his marvellously beautiful head down to my knees, and whispered low some few strange inaudible words—words of incantation, words of magic: he could afford to be humble, for he was like a king who knows how mighty he is and how supreme. And then his lips were very red, as on fire. . . .

All at once I shook myself free with a hissing intake of the breath, and gently extricated myself from his embrace.

"What, my Queen of the Icy Caverns!" he said in sport, with his eyes fixed upon mine. "Has some thought of death come to make you afraid?"

"No; I was thinking of Martha."

His bantering humour left him at once.

"Oh! for once in our lives surely we might learn to think only of ourselves," he said, and his tone showed that he was vexed with me.

"And have you found that lesson so very hard to learn?"

"That's unkind of you," he whispered, and closed my mouth with a kiss. . . .

"And now I have no more love left, not even for my husband. Not that I love another, not that Witold has made me suffer torments beyond endurance. No: I am merely unable to feel anything else in the world save pain. The very thought of him is a torture."

As she spoke, I bowed my head very low.

"It may be that there is some world in which Kant's 'categories' do not hold, where we are out of Space, out of Time. I believe it is so. Sometimes space does not exist for me: I have the power to see all those he has loved with him in one place. There are moments, too, when time does not exist for me: I can see them all together in one instant— both those that have been and those that are to be; *yes, those that are to be,* Janka."

From under her brows she threw me a questioning glance, and went on:

"But I can see, I can fancy nothing, save under the mental form of Pain. Yes, and I have thus discovered a new 'category'!"

It were difficult to say why, just at that moment, I remembered Wieloleski and his discovery that land-owning was also a "cate-

gory," and this put me in a humour of pleasantry that it was not easy to shake off.

"Looked at through this prism of Pain,"
she continued, "the sun itself is black, the most
superb flowers in the Red Garden turn to
tongues of flame, and the cistern filled with
flowers of bliss changes into an infinite, infinite ocean of blood."

She looked round, and shuddered.

"Pray, Janka, do not go to bed to-night; do
not leave me alone during the dark hours.
Truly, I cannot remember when he went out.
I think he was not at all at home to-day."

"Yes, he was; he dined with us."

She passed her hand over her brow.

"You are right, but it doesn't matter. At
any rate, he will not be here till morning.
Janka, do not sleep in your room!"

By this time it is impossible for me to endure the sight of Martha. She fills me with
such mystic awe that I am ready to shriek
aloud with dread of her. I feel as though I
were the cause of all her afflictions, as if it
were I who have marred her life. Her eyes
hurt me—those great dark-blue, sorrowful

eyes. But all the same it must make no difference to her; to her who—

On returning from the office, I stepped in
to Mme. Wildenhoff's, to see about the room
Gina spoke of. At any price, I must get away
from here. I want never to see either her or
him any more.

Mme. Wildenhoff was a little paler than
her wont; she looked out of sorts, and com-,
plained that her head ached. I understood
that something had gone wrong between him
and her. And again my heart was crushed
with fear. Only when I looked at her did I
remember that she likewise— . . . I had for
the time being entirely forgotten that fact.
My first impulse was to flee her; but Mme.
Wildenhoff retained me against my will. She,
I think, has not made any definite guess; but
the other!

"I must confess to you," she began, "that
all I have made you think of me is untrue—a
mask of mine, a mannerism, an empty theory.
All women are at their heart's core exactly
alike; during all their life they follow one
thing alone, and perish in pursuit of it."

"You mean love?" I questioned, trying
clumsily to feign indifference.

"Yes. That is the one thing. It is our fate; if not the first thing that we pursue, it is always the last that we give up. There is no help for it—none. We may be all our life forcing upon ourselves the conviction that we have the same rights as men, and are capable of bearing the same amount of liberty as they; but there must come a moment when, for that one true love, we most willingly give up all its counterfeits."

"But you have, Madame, the comfort to know that men too are liable to a similar reaction. When quite sated with freedom, the very greatest profligates will settle down to a married life."

"Only for a short while, and then they begin all over again, and return to their favourite pastime. . . . Why, take Imszanski, for instance; you surely know him well. . . ."

My face flushed up as red as fire, but I undauntedly raised my eyes to hers. She, on encountering my gaze, blushed, too. Once more I felt an uneasy flutter at my heart.

She burst into a sudden transport.

"I love, I love, and without any return!— Oh, how unlike me, is it not?"

Whereupon she laughed hysterically, and

then shed tears, tearing at her handkerchief with her teeth. She was waiting for me to put her some questions, that she might be able to confide her sorrows to me. I thought I should soon be likely to go mad.

At last Gina came in. She took me to Idalia, a fairly well-known pianist, who returned here from Paris a year since.

The room was very much to my taste; so was Idalia. There, all is tranquil and artistic. There I find nothing of that monstrous life which hurts me so—that lie which I feel here in my eyes as they look, in my mouth as it speaks!

Now I have left the Imszanski's for good. Even for my nature, life with them was too exquisite a torment.

Martha, according to her custom, has understood everything but let nothing come to her as a surprise. Nor has she in any way altered her behaviour towards me.

When I told her it was too far for me to go from her house to the office, she never asked why, during close upon three years, I had not noticed the distance. She appears not to know that I am aware she has no more trust in me.

When, for the last time, I entered my room,

in which there was but little change (for only a few of my things had been brought to their flat) I burst out crying. Martha stood by my side, grave and mournful.

Later, too, at the moment of my departure, there came to me a horrible pain of unbounded bewilderment, that took me, so to speak, suddenly by the throat. All this was, I thought, so heart-rending, so incomprehensible!

Imszanski was speaking to the porter who helped the man-servant to take my things downstairs. Then I asked Martha: "Don't you—don't you think it were better for me to die now, this instant?"

A smile dawned in her face, which she averted to hide it.

"No," she said; "there is no need. Nothing comes to me unexpectedly now. . . . And latterly I have found an enemy—in myself besides."

Quietly, daintily, she kissed me on the lips, and then, with a gracious gesture, gave her hand to Imszanski, who was going out to take me to my new abode.

I sit for a long time, spending the evening with Imszanski. And I enjoy myself. Al-

though I do not for one instant forget her,
that graceful melancholy woman, who now is
wandering through the magnificent apartments of her lonely dwelling, always awaiting
him, though she knows he will not come, and
at the slightest noise rushing to the ante-
chamber, listening with her ear close against
the door, and her brain on fire with excitement.   But the billows of undisturbed stillness are beating all around her. . . . And
then she goes back to her rooms, and seats herself upon an easy chair, and again upon a
lounge, trying to fall asleep; and to keep herself from sobbing aloud, she bites her fingers
hard. . . . And in a little while she goes once
again and listens at the ante-chamber door.
For now I am no longer by her side; now she
is quite, quite alone; and so cruelly abandoned!

Not for an instant do I forget all this; and
yet I enjoy myself.   The faint bitterness of
this tragedy gives, I suppose, an additional
flavour to our amorous and delightful dal-
liance.

Witold would prefer not to speak of the
subject, which I nevertheless bring forward
again and again.

"But tell me now, how could you behave with such abominable baseness, forcing yourself into Martha's life so? For you married her under downright compulsion: I well remember that she resisted with all her might. Were you at the time really in love with her?"

"She attracted me extremely, and I was puzzled by her great love for virginity. Never before had I found any woman with the instinct developed to such a degree. And I was then in a romantic, an idealistic, a Platonic mood, with which Martha harmonized to perfection."

"Well, and how was it that this mood of yours came to alter so quickly?"

"I found Martha just a little disappointing: and even at the time when I married her I was quite sure that she could not satisfy me for long. All that alluring mystery of her ascetic philosophy of life merely proceeded from anæmia and poverty of temperament."

"Witold! Witold! do go back to her again. For remember; I shall never love you as she does."

"No, I will not; I will not," and he gathered me in his arms: "I will not leave you, nor would I, even if you came to hate me.

Besides: what, in this whole affair, has pained Martha most? Why, it is your leaving us. She is always sitting in your room; and she very often talks of you, and wonders why you don't come."

I had reached the conclusion that all Witold had said was but of a piece with the rest of Martha's behaviour, studiously correct in regard of him: but I have got a letter from her to-day.

"Come to me, Janka, come! Do not bear me more ill-will than I bear to you. Remember that everything in our relations is still just as it was before. The memories are too deep-rooted; I cannot—— Once I loved you even more than——

"I await you. M."

I shall go to her to-morrow.

She received me, clad in a black dressing-gown, with grey borders and a silver fringe. I found it hard to conceal the painful impression that I felt. We talked together in a friendly way for about an hour.

With some air of mystery, she explained to me the idea she had of fitting up a boudoir entirely in mourning. "It might be made quite ornamental. The walls hung with crêpe, the furniture of black wood, uphol-stered with white plush, crosses of silver and of ebony, standing and suspended chandeliers of silver, a profusion of such flowers as are used to dress a catafalque, a large table in the centre, covered with a black cloth. And the boudoir lit with wax tapers only."

She then showed me an album bound in black leather, with a silver cross that stood out in relief on the cover.

With an embarrassed smile, she explained its contents to me.

"Here I have placed all Witold's loves, in chronological order," she said, and the very sound of his name made her blush hotly. "The number looks very great indeed, but this is because I have in many cases several por-traits of the same person."

I looked it over for a time, enthralled and captivated by these faces, each of a different type, some laughing, some grave, some pa-thetic, others comical or exotic or common-place, these full of fire, those ethereal-look-ing; many attired in the strangest raiment, or posing in voluptuous attitudes, and stretching out their half-nude limbs with serpent-like grace,—all these surrounded with Oriental magnificence: and again exquisite women, very *lady-like* in their British stiffness, and the sexless elegance of their tailor-made dresses simple but striking. A multitudinous chaotic assembly of many a style and many a nationality, down to one monstrously sensual negress, no doubt a singer in some music-hall.

"Since you have been away," she said, "it has been a custom with me to pore over this album. Those different faces remind me of the different periods of my life. I possess but few belonging to the old times of Witold's love-making; but of those he loved since he married, not one is wanting here. Some of them I purchased myself."

"That," I observed, "was of old a custom of yours. I remember well how as a girl the collections you liked best to make were post-cards with photographs of handsome actresses."

"Oh, but that was quite different," she replied with a shake of the head. "I feel such a pleasure in gloating over this collection!"

"Yes, the pleasure you take in self-inflicted torture!"

"No, not even that. You see, I gaze at those beautiful faces, those full red voluptuous mouths, those white rounded shoulders, so pleasantly smooth and soft; I look through the garments and see the colour of the flesh beneath: and each of these women I fancy delirious, swooning in his arms; and so I feed my mind with the thought of their delight in him—or perhaps (I am not quite sure which) of his delight in them!"

Her nostrils were quivering. She settled herself in her soft-cushioned seat, and closed her eyelids; they were red with tears.

On one of the first pages of the album I found Mary Wieloleska, clad as an Algerian girl, blithe and blandishing, and far better-looking than in reality. Towards the end there were about a dozen photographs of Mme. Wildenhoff, and one—a small one—of that French actress whom we had seen at Lipka's restaurant. The thought flashed upon me—a very unflattering one assuredly—that she had already placed me there too; but, sitting as I was by Martha's side, I could not possibly look at the last page. Besides, she herself held the album, and showed me no

photographs after those of Mme. Wildenhoff
and of the French actress.

The same thought occurred to us both at
once, and it cast over us the shadow of a
moody silence.

She laid her head on my bosom, and closed
her eyes with an expression of the utmost
fatigue.

"Don't go on like that," I said to her soothingly. "That way madness lies, and you
might easily get there."

"Oh, that is very likely. Indeed I wish I
may. Oh, to lose memory, and consciousness,
and all feeling!" And then: "For I am everlastingly wringing my own heart, Janka!" she
added, very sorrowfully.

Silently, I stroked her long dishevelled hair,
and all the while, with tender craving and
emotional entrancement, my mind was revert-
ing to Witold.

"Are you my husband's paramour by now?"

It was with some surprise that I was aware
the question evoked in me a reaction of out-
raged dignity. But I choked down the feeling, and unembarrassed, though with downcast eyes, I answered, in a low voice:

"No, not as yet."

"That is better. You may then presently become his wife."

Her mouth was slightly twitching. She has that most unpleasant habit of melting with compassion over her own woes.

"Only, please, Martha, not death! Don't let us hear about death!"

"I am in a very bad way."

"The idea! You always have been so terribly afraid to die; you told me so. Do you remember?"

"Oh, but it's quite another thing now!— Afraid of death, I?—No, I desire it with all the desire of my wretched heart. Yes, I desire it that you may become his wife, that you may yourself fathom the depths of the tortures I have gone through, and bask (as I am doing) in the beams of the bliss they give; that you, like me, may taste the delight of them by cupfuls brimming over!—Yet more, yet more! —May you quaff your fill of wormwood, till you overflow with it!—be suffocated with the mortal scent of those flowers of his—drink in their odoriferous delight and the poisonous steam of them, even to agony, even to death! —May I be avenged, when you are forced to yield him up to another! And may the knowledge that even death itself is no sufficient expiation, make the bitterness of your last hour bitterer still. . . . Oh, God!"

She hid her face in her hands; she was trembling all over with the violence of her spasmodic outburst. Finally, she fell on her knees before me, covering my hands with kisses that I felt burning hot.

"No, Janka, these words of mine are not true: they are lies,—lies! There is no longer any hatred at all, nor any thirst for vengeance: there is none—I love you! . . . I shall die, that you may be happy—in his Red Garden— and that he too may be happy by your side. Don't you believe me? Won't you look into my heart? My only wish is for your happiness: beyond this, I have no wish whatsoever. . . . I humble myself at your feet thus, see! and bless you that in your turn you have taken away from me what to me is dearer than life itself; that you have poured into the cistern of my bliss the last drop of that nectar which inebriates unto death. I love you: it was Christ, was it not? who gave the command that we ought to love our enemies. . . . Hear me!—I am dying that you may be happy with him. I wish you all happiness. I want to receive death at your hands,—your beautiful hands, so soft to caress. I would not have you feel any twinge of remorse: I would you could kill me, and yet not know that my death has cleared the way for your triumphal chariot.—Oh, Janka! be happy!"

Her head fell back; her eyes closed fast, and her teeth were clenched, showing between her half-open lips.

"Slay me, Oh, slay me!"

Now she has fainted. I lift her up, and lay her limp and lifeless body on a couch.

The purple chamber grows dark in the gathering twilight.

III

A CANTICLE OF LOVE

"I EXPECT you will be here in a day or two; so this letter will never be sent. I am writing only to be alone with you this evening; and if I write it, it is but for my own sake.

"It is an autumn evening, most marvellously fine. I want to be with you. For I do love you, my dear, my only one!

"The earth is black, the sky is blue, the gloom is deepening. A little while since, Idalia handed me a letter from you; and now I am in a vein of tenderness. I will not even chide you for excess of openness in your naturalistic way of expressing your desires. There are moments when I can pardon everything. . . . I want to show that I love you, very truly and very much. The days of my ill-humour, the days of my dark misgivings, have passed away now, and the days of bright vision are come. This very morning I was saying to Idalia that I should advise her not to fall in love, for I am so far gone that I cannot fancy myself capable of loving anybody but you. . . .

"I should be a hundred times better to you than I am, if I were not afraid. For now, since you made your confession, I feel afraid lest you should get the upper hand: and in love, I do not believe that two can both be on an equal footing. And if I but yield up to you one jot of my rights—anything whatever —you show no generous feeling at all, but triumph over my self-abasement, as if it were abjection. Witold, have some little generous feeling; allow me to rest for a moment from this eternal watch I must keep over myself; let me love you in peace, were it only for a short while.

"Again and again, the painful thought is borne in upon me, that—this time as well as the last—the pleasure of meeting you will not compensate for the pain of longing when apart. My mind misgives me, too, that you might have come to-day, but did not: 'Why? you really didn't know,' as once before. I make no reproaches, but am a little piqued, and may once more go off, as I did last spring,

in order to get away from you, so that you
may learn better how genial, how clever, how
incomparable I am.

"There is no doubt about it: you love me
more than I love you. And if I say this so
frankly, that is only because it is not absolutely true. Now I am going to tell you a
most important thing, which I never yet
pointed out to you quite clearly, and to which
you have to give a direct answer. So, attention!—We might love each other equally, but
I love you less: why?—Because you do not
make yourself in the least uneasy about my
love, neither as to what you confess you have
done, nor (which is far more important) as
to the disposition you may be in at the time.
You have done what you have done, and you
feel as you feel; and you find frankness a more
convenient thing than concealment. And so
I must constantly keep your love at high
pressure, forcing my disposition, and not
showing what I really feel. Now this is unjust. Once you said to me: 'Never allow me
to get the upper hand, for I should make a
slave of you: as soon as Martha became my
slave, I ceased to love her.' I then resolved
to hold my position of superiority, became

more secret, less natural; and all that is in
me of feebleness, abasement, poverty of spirit,
—the *ewig Weibliches*—I most carefully
locked up and kept to myself alone, in order
to provide our love with a longer existence,
which surely concerns you as much as myself.
If now I told you not to press your cheek
against my dress, nor humble yourself before
me, because I cannot love where I do not honour—you would begin to sulk and to tell me,
with the air of a cross sullen child, that you
are the one of us two who loves most, and that
I have shown myself a selfish girl.—In my
opinion, the preservation of our mutual love
is the affair of us both, and like an altar on
which we should both of us sacrifice absolute
sincerity, especially as concerns passing dispositions, and more especially such as imply
self-abasement; we must play a part, wear a
mask, and keep strictly to ourselves all such
grievances as might lower one in the eyes of
the other. So I ask you, who know this well
by the experience of your own life: am I right
or not? If I am, then: Do you intend to make
me love you as much as you love me, or would
you lower the level of your love to that of
mine? That is: will you bear the burden of

constant watchfulness with me, or do you deliberately consent that I should set it aside?—
Answer me that. And do not forget all about it in ten minutes.—And, in spite of all, I love you very much.   J. D."

Witold returned only yesterday. He was at a great shooting party in Klosow, where he was obliged to go, as a proof of his friendly relations with Janusz, and so put a stop to rumours rife among the neighbouring gentry that Martha and he were separated. Once I forbade Janusz to shoot hares; all that has long ago been forgotten, and now he astonishes everybody by his skill as a marksman. The Past—is the Past!

These few last years, which have not told at all upon Witold, have changed Janusz beyond recognition. He has married "a young lady from the country," and grown fat and rubicund and common; he has four sons, of whom he is excessively proud: Witold brings me news that he is expecting a fifth shortly. The former wild primitiveness of his nature only shows itself now on his occasional visits to town, when he carouses and revels furiously, in company with Witold.

As to his sister Martha, she has been in Germany for about six months, staying at a sanatorium for nervous patients. She is allowed neither to receive any letters nor to write any. We only now and then get news from the doctor, saying that she is better, and will soon be able to return to her home. She is, as the kindly German has the politeness to add, always pining after her husband and her son. The latter is being brought up with Janusz's boys, and the country air must have a very salutary influence upon his system.

I took but a very short leave this summer, spending nearly all the time in town with Witold, and leading something like a domestic life; for he shows himself in my case very particular about keeping up appearances. I wonder why, in his former relations with Mme. Wildenhoff, he never cared a fig for them! Perhaps he means, by taking such care, to show how much he esteems me.

He read my letter through, but made no comments on it; he suddenly remembered some incident at the shooting-party, telling it to me. And then he set about caressing and kissing me: he had been wanting me so very, very badly!

"But answer my question, Witold," I said.

"How can I? I don't know," was his answer, as he ardently kissed my inquisitorial eyes.

"Janka, is not this the best answer of all?"

He is always like that. My looks set us apart, his kisses unite us together.

But I am wrestling, held in the grip of my love, as a kite that soars above the clouds wrestles with the string held by a boy at play!

Idalia is not averse to having company at her lodgings, where I have met several characters in the artistic world.

Wiazewski cannot hear "Bohemianism." Yet in spite of this he not unwillingly comes, too, to see us, and to "observe."

"Look well at all those men," he says. "For the most part ill-shaped, ill-favoured, sitting in corners and smoking cigarettes, and paying no attention whether ladies are present or not. All of them sceptical and pessimistic, taking no interest in any but exaggerated views, and in most deadly earnest about all their convictions. That is the type of men I most abhor. If intelligent, they grow narrow-minded; and, if dull, utterly impossible in society. You have surely noticed that the greatest fool, so long as he has no convictions of his own, may be a very nice gentlemanly fellow."

"And what about the women?"

"They are less unendurable. They don't talk of feminism, they don't approve of women's emancipation, and (best of all) they practise it very effectively indeed. They have a great deal of intuition, but for all that—and luckily so—not a grain of conscious experience."

"Whom do you like best of all?"

"Miss Janina Dernowicz."

"I was asking about artists; I am not one."

"Ah, I see.—Artists? The prettiest is Miss Wartoslawska, whom I have known for a good long space of time. But just now she is far from looking as well as usual.—Why does not Owinski come here with her now?"

"Owinski?" I hesitated for a moment. Then: "Well, the engagement has been broken off for a month," I said.

"Has it? Yes, I had heard something about his being affianced to some one, but fancied it was only gossip. . . . Why, he seemed to be a very passive sort of fellow, and bore the yoke meekly enough."

"I don't know who is responsible for what has taken place."

"Oh, you have but to look at her, and you can't help guessing. . . . Besides, women always love longer and more deeply. It is through love that they attain their highest degree of culture; and I must acknowledge that, so far as culture goes, they have outstripped men; a woman's instinct stands higher than the wisdom of a man."

"Why, Stephen, from where have you got this attitude of benevolent optimism towards woman?"

"Of tragical pessimism, I should say," he answered, gayly, but then was lost in a brown study.

How am I to know? Very likely this also is love. And a good thing, too, that it came to me: I was so lonely then and so crushed with longing!

Now and then I enjoy emotions of super-human delight, of ecstatic bewilderment. And then again there flutter about me, like black moths, certain bitter self-reproaches for the past, and maddening apprehensions as to the future.—Really, it is too ridiculous! . . .

As if there could be anything worse than the sepulchral monotony of my life, as it formerly was!

And yet I know—I *know!*—that this is not happiness: that this romantic adventure of mine will have no morrow.

Put an end to it? I cannot; for just now the man is as necessary to me as the air I breathe. But some time or other I shall not love him any more; and then I shall hold it as a sacred duty to pay him for his deeds in the past by my future conduct.

And she, this my poor love! stands here, gazing with eyes full of frantic terror at her end, that will and must come some day!

The keynote in the tragedy of woman's life is the fact that her need for permanent love stands in contradiction with men's instincts and with their interests. Wiazewski calls this her "higher culture." I think that Schopenhauer's justification of this need as simply a case of design in nature is far more convincing. For how can we see any superiority in an instinct that we find equally developed in the most refined *inamorata* with her deep emotions, and in the average middle-class woman, all given up to passivity and routine?

After Owinski had engaged himself to a
new *fiancée,* he would still, in the beginning,
come at times and call upon Gina.

She would receive him with a smiling face
and serene looks, and endeavour to delude him
into thinking that no change had taken place,
and that, if he said he had come back to her,
she would be neither surprised nor dismayed.
. . . She would talk about things which had
interested them both; about her paintings and
his poems. Together they read books, treat-
ing of the Beautiful, and Life, and Love.
Once he said that he could not come to see
her the next day, as his intended was to arrive
in town; she took it as quietly as if he had an-
nounced his mother's or his sister's arrival.
But, though they still called each other by
their Christian names, they no longer kissed,
not even at parting.

On one occasion, she asked him to read her
one of his poems; a thing he was always willing to do. She listened, adapting to each
changing phrase of his mind as she had used
to do, and following every flash of his eye.—
Now, there were many works of his with
which she was not acquainted: formerly, she
had been the first to read anything he wrote

With a composed and tranquil mien, she listened even to the love-song, written for "the other." Of course, they were the output of the reaction which had set in: the magic power of innocence; the first confession of love from the untouched lips of one ignorant of life; the return of his springtime, of his youth, of his ideals. . . . Gina had great self-control. At the end of one such poem, she handed him a love-song of the old times, written three years before, and under her enchantment. And this too he read aloud as he had read the others; and, roused to enthusiasm by the very music of the lines, showed a fire too evidently, alas! out of all connection with the object which had once inspired them.

Like a tune sunk deep in memory in bygone days, the words at once brought all the past before her: it rose up, plainly visible to her mind's eye. The vision was agonizing, and the dismay of it made her raise her hands to her throat, as if to prevent the outburst of lamentation that now tore her bosom, as if she had been a feeble child, long and unjustly ill-treated. For she knew not how long, she wept like one distraught, even forgetting that he was present, and only aware that all her universe had given way, was broken to pieces, crumbled to dust, annihilated.

Some one took her tenderly in his arms, smoothed her hair, kissed those moist, red, tear-swollen eyes of hers.

She felt it, and this act, meant to comfort her, seemed to her harder than all to bear. It was a kiss of pure sympathy for suffering, of mere humanity, a last farewell kiss.

The anguish she felt stifled her; she could not breathe,—till her pain tore its way out of her breast in a tempest of weeping.

Then, as in a nightmare, she heard his steps farther, farther away, and the sound of the door closing upon him. She knew it was closing upon him for ever; she knew that he would not return.

And then there came a time when she crept to his feet, like some poor beast that its master has driven away; and when, no longer admitted to his house, she loitered about for him in coffee-houses and in the street, and importuned him with letters incessantly. Whichever way he went, he was doomed to behold that face, pale as a spectre, and those eyes, so reproachful and so full of entreaty!

At present Owinski salutes her distantly, as

he would salute some slight acquaintance; but he gives no answer at all to any of her letters. Nor does he any longer call on people at whose houses there is any chance of meeting her.

When I look at Gina, Martha recurs to my mind directly.

Once I thought I had eaten of the fruit of the knowledge that there is neither good nor evil.

And nevertheless, there is a feeling here, in my heart,—a silly persistent feeling,—that all that has happened is evil, most evil, whereas it might just as well have been good.—An adventitious otherness; circumstances, or possibly dispositions, make all the difference. . . .

Yes, but I constantly see those eyes,—those pure dark-blue eyes, which had not merited for her such pangs as she has suffered—and the curve of that mouth, her tiny crimson mouth, set hard with pain, and always ready to burst out into lamentations.

She sometimes appears to me as a fiend, whom I hate for her obstinate will to suffer, for the childish and insensate whim of posing as a victim, for her attitudes and her love to

gloat over herself. She comes with black
wings and fluttering white hands; with a beg-
gar's impudence, she opens out her mourning
weeds and shows me her bosom; beneath her
white transparent flesh, I can see her purple-
coloured heart. And she points to it. It is
misery that has stained it so deep a red, filling
it with red fire; for there is not a single drop
of blood in it any more.

And she strokes that heart with dainty
relish, and smiles on me malignantly.

I—am suffering remorse!

To differentiate between good and evil is
far from wise. This is why my ethical principles are of such primitive simplicity. All
my culture exists only in my brain; what is
emotional in me remains elemental and primitive, full of stupid sentiment and of scruples.

And therefore it is that I am so unlike other
women, whose great characteristic is that their
feelings are cultured.

At times, when I see him afar, standing out
from amongst the crowd, splendid in shape
and wonderful in beauty, I have a sense of
pride that he is mine—my own! Neither a
pet cat nor a dog, neither a parrot nor a

canary: a man of the world, tall, refined, in life's prime. And this marvellous creature belongs to me. It is truly hard to realize this; and my brain whirls with pleasure at the very thought of such a possession.

When sitting by my side, he loses that charm of his, so extremely rare and of no less value,—the charm of aloofness. He is mine assuredly, my Witold. I know him well, I know him by heart. Never anything but by fits and starts; incorrigible in his defects, which are exceedingly hard to bear; obstinate and childish; his mind consisting of two or at most three strata, the uppermost of which alone contains a little gold; and under this you may root and dig all your life long, and never find anything but sand, and sand, and sand for ever!—But why do I always want to find things out, and go deeper and deeper?

When he kisses, it is as if he were drinking the blood out of me. I turn pale, and am weak and inert—ever more and more inert. In his arms I melt, or am like a flower drooping and dying in the sunbeams. I have not the strength even to raise my eyelids; it is as though the lashes had grown together.

But—and this is an odd thing—I never

yield beyond a certain point, not determined by any resolve or will of mine, but by instinct and instinct alone. A moment comes when there surges up within me as it were a cold and ironically smiling energy; with one gesture, I repulse that creature full of intemperate desire, enchanting though he is in his thoughtless waywardness.

He always goes away humbled, vanquished, and concealing under the hearty kindness of a farewell kiss the gathering hostility of an everlasting antagonism.

For indeed I have never yet been his "paramour," in any sense of the word used by Martha, when she questioned me.

Yet, when victorious, I at times wish that I had been defeated. Truly, I cannot understand myself. But I do not so much as attempt to strive against this something within me that can even overcome the natural bent of my temperament.

It is conceivably the instinct of self-preservation, which has in woman, through the immemorial working of heredity, been turned in one and only one special direction, antagonistic to unchastity. The ideal woman would prefer death to what is called *shame,* would she not?

And I also possess this involuntary and automatic tendency, instinctive yet purposeful; and in me it is only very partially blunted by the force of sober reason. But this explains well why my bias towards emancipation has its source and finds its scope chiefly in the intellectual sphere.

Last evening I spent some time in Gina's studio. I was glad she had asked me to come, for last night there was something or other on at Witold's club, and I do not like to pass my evenings alone now. I fear my own thoughts, which are never so profound as in solitude and by night. This activity of my mind sometimes exceeds my limited strength to bear it. And when I note that there is in this some resemblance between myself and Martha, I again hear her prediction of vengeance ringing in my ears.—There are moments when, oh, how weak, how very weak I feel!

Although I have known Gina for a long time, our relations are always on a strictly formal footing. When we meet at a common friend's, her behaviour is almost distant;

when she is playing the part of hostess, she is
not only courteous, but eager to show courtesy; and this difference in her bearing is very
marked. At home, she is seldom gloomy, will
not let the conversation flag for an instant,
shows me her paintings, her albums, new
periodicals and books; makes me most delicious black coffee; and is incessantly moving
about, light-footed and supple, with lithe and
snake-like motion, dressed in a long dark gown
with trailing skirts, glittering with her gold
ear-rings and her metallic belt, amid the
easels and canvasses and stools of every shape,
and all the admired disorder of her studio.
And she tactfully avoids talking about herself, as she does not wish the least shade of
gloom to enter our conversation.

"Are you quite comfortable?" she inquires,
kindly. "Please don't stand on ceremony, but
sit down on this ottoman: very cosy, believe
me. Let me put this skin under your head—
the softest fur; as soft as silk. Now isn't it
nice to rest on?"

She fetches me a tiny stand, and places a
cup of coffee upon its lower shelf, with tea-
cakes and a tiny glass, so that I have everything close at hand.

"Now, a little drop of liqueur; that will do nicely, won't it?"

In her studio a beautiful soft red twilight prevails. The lamp, well shaded, glows in a corner upon a low table. The easels throw black lines, long-drawn, big and grotesque, upon the upper parts of the walls. A glazed roof, which forms the greater part of the ceiling, looks like black velvet, framed in white with pink flowers along the frames.

Gina is to some extent an imitator of Costenoble. The last sketch made by her for a very large painting represents a man, with head thrown back in a pose of fatuous triumph, while at his feet a woman, instinct with subtle delicacy, suggests by her attitude the coils of a writhing serpent.

The sketch, as a whole, is melodramatic, and not very convincing. I prefer Gina as Gina to Gina as an artist.

I love to look at her, sitting close to me, reclining in that big easy-chair, with her long white hands carelessly dangling from the arms of her chair, forming as beautiful and as dainty a picture as any artist could create.

"Won't you come with me to a concert on Thursday next?" she asks. "Ileska is to recite a poem by my ex-fiancé. He will certainly be there—and she too. I have not yet seen her, and should like to do so. There will also be piano and vocal music. Not a bad programme."

"Of course I shall be much pleased, but—have you considered . . . ?"

"Oh, don't worry, I shall manage all right. . . . It can surely make no great impression upon me."

She smiled.

"I should not have forced myself on you; but since Lola Wildenhoff's departure, I have no one but you to do me this service. I am now so very easy to upset; and any want of tact jars upon me so!"

"I fancied that you were on pretty intimate terms with Idalia."

"Not at present. True, she is still, as she always was, as discreet as can possibly be. But she has too much sentiment and sympathy—far too much; and that is annoying and mortifying. You, so tranquil, so quiet, so entirely unmoved, act on my nerves as a sedative. I can talk with you even more openly than with Lola."

"Oh, have you heard from her?"

"Yes; I received one letter. She has left the Riviera, and is in Paris now, where she intends to winter along with her husband. Wildenhoff has won a good deal of money, playing at Monte Carlo; and both of them are now spending it, each of them apart."

"And her nerves, how are they?"

"In perfect condition. She has left all her tears in the sea behind her. . . . That woman has an uncommonly happy disposition——"

Here followed a short but mournful pause, broken by the entrance of Radlowski, a painter who had been her fellow-student in Munich.

He noticed that my complexion was strikingly out of the common, and begged I would sit for my portrait.

Witold thinks that, of all the women he ever knew, I am the most intelligent. Before he made my acquaintance, he had been climbing up a regular ladder of emotions, of which Martha had formed the topmost rung. I, it appears, form a sort of synthesis of all his loves; I am at the same time the most beloved humanly speaking, and as a woman the most desired of all. He would not have me other

than I am in any way.—As to this last, I wish
I could say the same of him.

And yet I would not exactly have him
changed—rather transformed and become another person. It seems that to be as lack-
brained as an animal is not sufficient: one must
besides have some primitive instincts, one
must have some vigour. . . . What I need
now, perforce and irresistibly, is matchless
strength—the strength of a hurricane, of a
cyclone, of some great natural force let loose.

He loves to talk with me on intellectual
matters. "No one can understand his soul so
well as I."

Silent and with eyes cast down, I listen for
some time to his commonplaces, uttered indeed in elaborately chosen words, and in a
manner not commonplace. And I ponder. I
gaze on him—on that mouth so perfectly
shaped, so intensely sweet, just a little faded,
it seems; and on those eyes which, beneath the
tawny lashes that shade them, are so bright
with the fever and the melancholy of lassitude, so full of the irresistible charm which
surrounds all that is coming to an end, though
you would have it remain as beautiful as only
youth's dream can be. And it is then—when

he has not the slightest inkling of what I feel
—that I love him most of all.

To-day I was sorry for him—sorry for all
those desires of his, doomed to burn themselves out, never any more to be kindled.

Acting on an impulse, I went up to him,
knelt with one knee upon his, put my hands
round his head, wonderfully soft and velvet-
like to feel, and then, turning his face up, I
gazed into those enchanting, nebulous eyes,
and said laughingly:

"Oh! in Heaven's name, Witold, why must
you talk about everything? You know well
enough that this is not what you were made
for, don't you? Pray remember that your one
strong point is love."

And then, for the first time, I kissed him
upon the lips, not waiting to be kissed by him.

He kissed me back again, but the kiss was
cool, brotherly.

"I regret," he observed, "that you show me
so little of your beautiful soul, and refuse to
acknowledge mine to be of a kindred nature.
Yet I understand so well your dreams of the
Arctic plains that you possess, of your
grottoes, glimmering green in the Northern
Lights; of your boundless and ever peacefully

slumbering ocean! I am for ever very near to you. . . ."

"That may be; but I am always very far away from you," I retorted, with an attempt at pleasantry. Then I whispered in his ear:

"Love my snows: for there are volcanoes seething beneath them."

At the words, his mouth fastened on to my neck, and he bit into my flesh with a kiss that gave me exquisite pain together with maddening delight.

My eyelids closed, my lips parted; I was about to faint. And I felt his mouth upon mine, and it was most sweet, with the savour of withered roses. And I drank of the crimson wine of his kisses, and it was strong as death.

And the crimson wine inebriated me.

But there came an evil moment. Was it Death, or was it Life, that then laid its cold hand upon my heart, and looked upon me with the eyes of wisdom?

The revulsion frees me, tearing me from his close embrace.—And I hated him, for he did not understand, and was unwilling to leave me. Yet, had he indeed left me thus, I should have resented it and longed for him!

No, never I shall be won by the graces of a young page with tawny eye-lashes, nor by the refined softness and subtlety of any art whatever. Strength alone can win me. As the cat carries off its little ones in its jaws, so let Him carry me away; and whithersoever he may take me, thither I shall go.

When we entered the concert-hall, it was already full. Gina was looking like a ghost.

We saw a good many people we knew, and several gentlemen came to present their respects. They were rather surprised to see Gina there, looked at her not without some tender interest, and seemed to scent a quarry.

Czolhanski, who as representative of his paper was sitting in the first row, also perceived us.

"Where is Mr. Witold?" he asked, looking round the hall. "I have been waiting for him, but he does not come."

"Unfortunately," I answered in a rather dry tone, "I am not in a position to enlighten you. However, if he has made an appointment with you, he may be expected to come."

In reality, however, I was quite sure that Witold would be absent. He had even advised me not to go to the concert, for he particularly wished me to be at home and with him. But I would not disappoint Gina.

"He has promised to be here for sure," repeated Czolhanski, as he went away.

I soon perceived Owinski walking up the central passage by the side of a lady in black attire, and no longer young. He was holding some tickets and endeavouring (in vain, shortsighted as he was) to find the corresponding numbers of the chairs. A pretty girl walked by the side of the lady in black; her dark eyes sparkled, and she was evidently much impressed by the important nature of the present performance. She spoke in a low tone to her fiancé, seeming to banter him on his embarrassment, and found the seats herself. They sat down at no great distance from us, on the farther side of the central passage.

Owinski left the ladies by themselves, and was returning to seek for something or other, when he happened to perceive us, as he passed by.

He changed colour slightly, and then approached to present his respects, kissing Gina's hand in silence. She, too, neither spoke a word nor lifted her eyes.

I congratulated him on having got so first-rate an artiste as Ileska to recite his poem; he answered in a few polite words, and withdrew.

There was a pause.

From his shapely tapering fingers, a tall young musician shook some heavy drops of mingled sounds, then sprinkled them about, and they grew ever more and more beautiful; now daintily rounded off—musical pearls, as it were—now broken and hard and angular like stones. Now thunder was heard; the hail pattered and rattled; and someone set up a low murmured wailing, and Gina hung down her head; then sunrise was triumphantly ushered in to the pealing of bells. And the slender artist in black evening dress went on, as before, slowly, drowsily, letting his blossom-like hands fall dropping upon the piano keys, soft as velvet under their touch, and suddenly, with a gesture too rapid to be seen, he shed a perfect shower of pearls round us, from the inexhaustible treasury of his kingly munificence.

Never yet have I at any concert been able to fall under the spell of music.

I listen, and I look. I may even feel dazzled. But, to be spell-bound! That requires seclusion, concentration. . . . There are times when I prefer a barrel-organ to a concert!

I coldly admired the astonishing technique of the young virtuoso, now playing in public for the first time, and the extraordinary charm he possessed, which was like hypnotism or magic. Gina sat enthralled and following each motion of his hands. She no longer cast any glances in the direction of her victorious rival; but sombre clouds were passing over her face, and she knit her golden brows and frowned heavily.

I glanced towards Owinski; but on the way my glance and a look from two black and most observant eyes crossed each other. So! *She* was scrutinizing Gina!

Silence came; and then a clapping of hands: the first-rate actress, who was thin and unattractive, had appeared upon the platform. She bent her head slightly in a formal bow, and looked round the hall from under gloomy brows. The audience waited, expectant and agitated.

A clear, distinct, cold voice was heard vibrating through the brilliantly lighted hall.

Then, as if preparing for a surprise, it

gradually grew mysterious, soft, and low. You thought of marble terraces, leading to subterranean vaults. The words seemed to take a sculptured form from her diction and utterance; their tones went lower, lower, lower still, became the muttering of a hushed lamentation, the rumbling sounds of a scarce audible curse, and the profoundest depths of the agony of death.

At intervals, Ileska would pause to cast her eyes down, and—in an ecstatic concentration of self-suggested rapture—wait while her wonderful voice, reverberated from the white and lofty walls, would echo back and fill her attentive ears. . . .

And then she would again open her great sombre eyes, and continue her recitation, inspired as it were by the sound of that strange voice of hers.

Indeed, she gave so much of her own special individuality to the poem she was so admirably reciting, that I did not at first recognize it as the work of Owinski. Gina, wrung with anguish, cast up her eyes and threw back her head, looking steadfastly into the glare of the electric candelabra, and blinking now and then, while a couple of tears were sparkling

in each outer corner of her eyes. She was trying to force them back into her heart by that
means. Ah, yes; I know that trick, I do, how
well! . . . But it was unsuccessful: indeed, it
does fail from time to time. Once two trans-
lucent pearls trickled slowly on to her tem-
ples, and were lost in the tresses of her brown
hair.

After Ileska, Mlle. Iseult Lermeaux, a
singer who would, according to Czolhanski,
be the great attraction of the concert, came
forward on the platform. Her figure, as soon
as I saw it, struck me as like some person
strangely familiar. Could it—could it be?
. . . No, the thing was incredible. I drew
my brows together, that I might concentrate
my attention and make sure. No, no; only a
fearful unaccountable pain had taken possession of me for an instant. It was Gina's own
pain that I felt, reflected within myself.—An
inexplicable bewitchment, that perhaps has its
reason in the drawn-out, lazy, lascivious,
dreamy notes of that song of a Southern land,
which she is singing: yes, it may be that.

No. No. NO.—It is she, none but she
. . . she beyond all doubt. Now I *know;* and
my knowledge is hell to me. Yes, I know all.

Ah! but she is fair, divinely fair! All the potency of the senses, all the exquisite refinements of art have come together to create this irresistible glamour that she spreads around her. No, no,—not a word! Those eyes, so amazing in their fairy-like beauty, and the long lashes that fringe them—those drowsy yet unfathomable eyes, like those of her whom King Cophetua loved so well! Yes, and it is her mouth, too—that wondrous, wondrous mouth, now pale and wan through excess of delights, either felt or known in dreams only. —But, Heavens! I can see this mouth pressed close to that other mouth, sweet beyond all sweetness,—that mouth fragrant with its terrible death-bringing scent, its scent as of withered roses! . . .

This—this is death!

Not so. Oh, no, it is not death: this is Life! Understand the truth.—It is life; behold it now: life in very deed.

You see now?—All is clear. It was for that reason that Czolhanski was awaiting him here. It was for that reason that he wished you not to come, and that, because you came, he stayed away.

Is—is not this yet Death?

No. It is Life: Life that, out of the accents of that voice, supremely melodious, drowsy, sleepy, yet replete with fire from an unfathomable abyss, out of the lazy, lascivious snaky curves of those limbs of hers; out of those glossy shoulders, so shapely, so slenderly fashioned, and of those outstretched naked arms, in hue like pale dead gold, has come forth towards you in all its hostile might!

Gina, lost in dreary amazement, was staring at me.

"What ails you? . . . Had we not better get away from here?"

We were both of us presently standing, frantic with pain, in the street which, lit up by the flaring windows of the great hall, was as bright as day.

"Let us go away—away!—Home? On no account.—Get drunk somewhere—lose my senses—shed some one's blood. . . ."

I was raving like one in a delirium.

"I beg you, Gina, come, come along—I can't bear any more!" I stammered.

She hesitated. "Unescorted and alone—to a night-restaurant?"

"What does it matter?"

"Better have made an appointment—somewhere—with Mr. Imszanski. . . ."

Then I burst into laughter. "Unescorted? Ha, ha, ha!" I roared, as we got into a four-wheeler. "Forgive me, but even so,—I fancy neither of us has much to lose!

"To Lipka's? I will not. No, I entreat you. No memories of things gone by—A hotel, any hotel!—or a first-rate night-restaurant. —Fast! As fast as horses can go! Faster, faster!"

Off they went, the great black half-starved horses. A few street-lamps flashed by in the dark night. A few jolts from the rubber-tired wheels made us sway about: and again it is all bright around. Oh! how I am tortured!

A cold blast blows, muddy pools splash, a drizzling rain sets in. . . . Oh, yes, yes; all this is very real: fact, not fiction.

Now a brilliantly lit doorway is before us; now a staircase, adorned with flowers and mirrors. . . .

Gina was eyeing me in astonishment, but she said not one word. She no doubt could not guess what had come over me; but, in her state of mind, the strangest occurrence must have seemed quite commonplace. And then, she no longer felt so much alone in her distress; beside my madness her state of tearful dejection seemed but a small matter.

The great saloon was filled as usual with specimens of the *jeunesse dorée,* with financiers, and with courtesans. We attracted a good deal of attention. I had assumed the gay mien of a girl desperately bent on fun, and looked about on all sides, with lively glances at everybody.—Several men spoke to me.

In the passage on to which the doors of the private supper-rooms opened, we were met by a young but full-grown satyr, who slipped his arm under mine, and looked into my face. And yet I did not cease to laugh. It was revenge I craved—debauch—oblivion of all!

Gina's terrified looks were expostulating with me.

"We have nothing to lose," I returned to their speechless appeal. And thereupon she too fell a-laughing strangely.

The creature whose arm was in mine kept chattering incessantly . . . about I know not what. A waiter respectfully opened the door of a small private room, and we all three went in.

"I presume, ladies, you have been at the play?" our gentleman inquired, having remarked the dresses we wore.

"Ha, ha!" I answered. "Right you are. Been at one play, and come to another." There was not less coarse ribaldry in my tones than in my words.

"That's first-rate.—The bill of fare, waiter! —What will you take?"

"To eat, nothing. We want to drink, to drink, to drink!"

"Very good!" he exclaimed, in a tone of pleased surprise. "Coffee and liqueur—cognac—champagne?"

"All right: anything and everything, my dear man!"

Several bottles were standing on the table. Our companion, having leisurely prepared a mayonnaise, set to munching the lobster with great relish, showing his white teeth in a grin. —Gina drank, but was mute.—I babbled incessantly, endeavouring to pass for a *cocotte*. We were a puzzle to the young man nevertheless, and his behaviour towards us was lacking in assurance.

"Do you know, Madame," he at last blurted out, addressing me, "it will be better fun if

we make a quartette. . . . I have an acquaintance in the saloon here: a capital fellow he
is."

Then, turning to Gina: "You also,
Madame," he said, "should have a little diver-
sion."

I protested very strongly.

"Not the least need for him; let him stay
where he is. You are what we want."

I held him back, putting my hands upon
his shoulders, and my face close to the animal
face of that unknown man.

He smiled, much flattered: his white teeth
gleamed.

"We shall not keep you long, if you wish to
leave us. But for the present, you have to
stay with us."

Some one—who could it be?—filled my
liqueur-glass with cognac again and again.
Presently, a crimson blood-red smoke began
to float from corner to corner of the small
cabinet, papered with red and gold, and filled
with the sound of his loud voice and the reek
of tobacco. All round me, everything was
afire and aflame.

He was drawing near; in every limb of
mine I felt his approach. His jaws, chewing

still, though his supper was over; his tiny
eyes, to which expectancy gave a phosphorescent glow; and the hot fulsome breath from
his gaping chops, embellished with splendidly shining fangs and incisors; and that blond
upstanding moustache of his:—I had all these
close to my face. He was unsteadily leaning
over, tilting his chair towards the sofa, touching and fingering the gauze trimming of my
bodice, and seeking my lips with his.

My brain, intensely excited, showed me
things as they were. But I half closed my
eyes, and looked at him through the lids as
though about to faint.

All would not do. . . . My mind was sober: its powers came into full play.

At that instant I drew back, and—with all
the force of my rage, hate, despair, and revenge—revenge for everything and for us all
—I dealt him a furious blow with my clenched
fist, right between those phosphorescent greenish lustful eyes!

He reeled, and fell along with his chair on
to the floor. Gina was at the door in a flash.

I flung down upon the table all the money
I had by me, and, slamming the door behind
us, rushed out in Gina's company.

No one was in the passage. I walked out of the saloon, my face by this time wearing an unconcerned expression. In the cloak-room we put on the hooded mantles we had taken to the concert. I went home, shorn of all my strength, and in a state of complete collapse.

An astonishing woman, that Gina! She never asked me for any sort of explanation.

"This explosion scene has done me good," was her indifferent and only comment.

From this day, I am her friend.

I have told Gina all about the whole business, from beginning to end. She said I was terribly naïve. "Things could not possibly have turned out otherwise." She advised me to forgive Witold. It was only if he had loved another that I could have had any cause for complaint. But such a passing connection as that! . . . Besides, I had no rights over him; and moreover, he was a man! . . . Owinski, too, had been several times unfaithful to her; and yet, though their relations had been very different from ours, she had always forgiven him: though indeed not without difficulty. . . . It was only now that the inwardness of suffering had come home to her. . . . Had he been willing, she would have agreed to his having a dozen others besides his wife!

"Never would *I* agree to such a thing as that," I replied. "If Witold gave me up for the love of some other woman, then I should at least be sure that my misery was of some service to others, and that there was on both sides equality of rights, since I too might have just as well fallen in love with another. . . . But if he is false to me for a mere plaything and to amuse himself with what does not mean any more to him than a good cigar, then I am absolutely unable to act, and quite defenceless against him. I shall never, never be able to do the same. And, between the measure of his guilt and of my retaliation for it, there is such huge disproportion as makes me ridiculous in my own eyes. . . . Why, when Roslawski forsook me, I was also most miserable: but in his behaviour at least there never was anything one whit so mean, so dirty, as this."

"I have not the slightest wish," returned Gina, "to impose my philosophy of life upon you."

He has excused himself; has assured me, even sworn that I am in error. I have refused to believe him. Women are hugely credulous, credulous in the extreme.

I have not seen him this whole week. He came here twice, but was denied entrance, as I ordered. I don't care for the forgiving system. I don't care to become like Martha. . . .

However, if I act thus, it is on principle only; in reality, I am tortured by his absence. My feelings incline me to believe that he says true. . . . Surely he cannot possibly be thus false to me.

I fear greatly lest, if he should come again . . .

No, no.—I am going to call on Wiazewski, who has of late been quite neglectful.

I started by complaining of things in general, and with but little of personal feeling. He has hitherto known nothing about my relations with Witold. And I am also ashamed of this love, in which I have been playing so ludicrous a part.

" . . . And to think of the years, the golden years of youth, gliding, gliding, gliding by, beautiful, but empty as some marble bath of ancient days! . . ."

"But I told you once that men of modern times do not care to bathe in those waters. They are too clear, too cold; they run with too swift a stream, and with too many, oh! far too many an eddy and deep hollow. Janka, they fail to *attract*."

"Let me say, Stephen, that I am unhappy, and therefore come to you. You, as a friend, have some responsibilities toward me; you can't get out of them. All that I am is going to pieces at this time; and I do not know whether life or death will come of the change which is taking place."

I had never yet yearned for Witold as at that moment, though I knew perfectly well that no one had done me the wrong which he had done.

"What about Helen?" I asked, with friendly interest.

"There again! I have been disappointed in her."

"What, she! Unfaithful to you? Can that be?"

"Ah, no! I, rather than she, have been at fault in that respect."

"Well then?"

"Well, what shall I say? I have broken with her."

Forsaken! She too had then come to swell the list, after Martha, Gina, and myself!

"That's horrible. She was so very much in love with you."

"Whereas I, alas! have a preference for women who care for nothing very much."

"Yet I know you have been moody of late."

"And you are right: yes, I have."

"Well, what was it that troubled your Olympian calm? The parting scene—tears—upbraiding?"

"*Pas le moins du monte.* She went away without uttering a word."

"Then what was it?"

"That I have simply lost my belief in the last dogma left to me from childhood. Everybody complains that women are too devoid of heart and brains and soul; and I now find that it is in vain I have sought for a woman bereft of those superfluous appendages."

"But Helen, as I understood, answered your ideal of a woman to perfection?"

"I fondly thought she did. Oh, you cannot imagine what I would give to meet a woman really soulless, primitive: you know,—a creature absolutely and bewilderingly unenlightened."

"Really, I quite dislike you to-day, Stephen. You are positively in bad form!"

"Please forgive me."

"What special mark of her culture has Helen given you?"

"Culture? That would have been by far too bad. Besides, it was something perhaps even worse: a mark of character, firm conviction."

"Up to now," he continued, "I had been quite satisfied with the girl; so, a few days ago, I proposed that she should give up her employment and come to live with me. Would you believe it? I met with a point-blank refusal. You fancy, perhaps, it was marriage she wanted, or something of that kind; and, word of honour! If she had, I would have taken her willingly. . . . Not at all. She told me sententiously that 'although she recognized free love, she never would be a kept woman!' What do you think of that, eh? Ha, ha! It's something astounding, isn't it?"

But I could not laugh. I sat silent, thinking

of many things, far more pained than amused.

Stephen continued: "A girl with such splendidly expressionless eyes of a bright azure, like a piece of water! No shadow of any yearning for the Beyond, no shadow of anything like intellect or brightness of thought! . . . By day they reflected the sun, her lamp in the evening, and my own eyes at night. They had the beautiful dead gleam of pearls. She might have been less pretty: with such eyes, she was pretty enough for me. And then, that slow, sleepy, brainless voluptuousness in her glance! And her white flashing teeth, too! I tell you, there is not a single spot or flaw in any one of them; her molars are like the molars of a ruminant, large and flat. She did, it is true, write me letters without necessity; but, through my influence and under my direction, she had come even to forget her alphabet. She truly gave me the impression (false as I know now) that she never thought at all.

"And that girl 'recognizes free love'! Such a surprise may well make one throw all the beliefs of one's life on the dustheap!"

All this talk of his seemed to me decidedly shallow and foolish. Why on earth was he trying, by means of that far-fetched theory of his, to justify the fact that the woman simply bored him?

He has now made up his mind to seek for his future Dulcineas amongst kitchen-maids.

"Dressmakers have decidedly too much culture for my taste," he said.

"I sincerely hope you may be successful," was my parting wish.

Witold, contrary to my expectations, has not yet called again. There is something going on that is beyond me, incomprehensible.

I am assailed by innumerable thoughts which make me turn pale with fear.

He, too, is possibly "seeking oblivion," as I was; but he is scarce likely to stop in time, like me. Moreover, his vengeance will not, like mine, be a more horrible pain than the injury itself.

He has a supremely great advantage over me, and the conditions of the struggle are the most unequal possible.

Will he delay coming for long? Is it conceivable that he has given me up for ever?

I was in tears all this evening.

Idalia felt it her duty to try and comfort

me. A kind, lovable girl she is. And she knows how to deal skilfully with "semi-tones" of every description. Her eyes are gentle, her face a little faded and careworn; there is something maternal about her.

"We take everything so very seriously, so very much *au tragique,*" she says. "And that, you see, puts us more in their power. We should analyse things less, and learn rather to glide over them. Analysis is a two-edged weapon: it easily turns and wounds you. Do endeavour to pass along with a cursory look about you, even with half-closed eyes; things will seem different at once. Don't cry any more: and if he should come, the servant is to let him in, is she not?"

"On no account; on no account;" I cried, in a fury.

"But why?" she murmured, gently stroking my hair. "Why? To let him in—that does not bind you in any way: you are free to act as you like. And why not hear what he has to say?"

"Because I have heard him already."

"And you would not believe him? You were not right in that. It is so easy to believe! . . . And whether the thing is true or not, what does it matter to you? What is true in some part of time may be false in some part of space; and *vice versa*. A fact is true, but only for the day. When he is beside you, and assures you of his love, you will have the greatest of all truths: the indubitable truth in the present. What took place before? . . . What is to come later? . . . Never mind: it is all the same!"

And I think she is in the right.

Every now and then Czolhanski comes and calls upon me. He came yesterday, too. This, I think, is rather too much. God! how I detest that man! . . . He enters, sits down, stays for three mortal hours, pays me a few compliments, lets out a few commonplaces about the lamentable position of a journalist: a man untidy, unshaven, rather dirty in his ways, and very pretentious: his finger-nails are in mourning and his hands always moist. No use to take up a newspaper, even to be more uncivil to him still: he will not take the hint and go. Once he wrote a sonnet to me! Journalism has evidently been the death of his poetical talent. But, Lord! what does it all matter after all? He *will* kiss my hands,

though I always beg him not to, he disgusts
me so. If I were in his place, I should go
and hang myself! And he—he is quite unaware of my feelings, and very much self-
satisfied.

Yesterday Radlowski came as well, and for
the first time, under the pretext of a message
from Gina. His company would be most
pleasant, for he is so very extremely young;
and his eyes sparkle like a diamond in the
sun, with a sort of delectation so lively that
it seems unnatural; painfully so. He has
again asked me to sit for my portrait.

I have promised: but I cannot—I cannot
as yet.

What is the reason of Idalia's playing so
very poorly to-day? She writhes and twists
herself to and fro at the piano, with more than
sensual affectation; she suddenly and convulsively coils and uncoils herself like a snake,
during the more brilliant passages: and she
goes on playing interminably, from dusk till
far, far into the deep, dark, never-ending
night.

And why is she doing so, this day of all

others, when all my strength to bear it has left me?

The longing, the pain I feel, is stifling, is strangling me: it bites at my throat, and I shudder to feel it cling round my feet like ivy, together with the thought of my blighted joys.

These I see lying on heaps of tropical flowers—lying in long rows, naked, asleep, and beautiful as dreams of what is past forever. . . . Over them there blows a gentle breeze, scattering the flower-petals upon their fairy-like forms; but it does not wake them from slumber. Only, from time to time, do their long black eye-lashes open and shut, slowly and rhythmically, as the silken wings of a fluttering butterfly. They are dreaming of their delights.

Say, O say! why does all this give me such infinite pain?

And then there always come to me haunting visions, which are my childhood! A dark outline of forest-trees; a perspective fading into infinite, infinite distance, and the clear waters wherein life lay hidden once upon a time. The vision stands, I know not how, for the times of my childhood. Music always renders concrete even the most abstract of things.

Something is tearing my soul; it is the impossibility of any delusion about . . .

Ah, do not, do not bite thus at my throat! . . . I cannot weep! . . . And do not make the sharp-edged music of the violin soft by the dark velvet touch of your smooth hand! . . . And do not, do not press my bosom so; my heart will burst! . . . And do not hug my body with that tender embrace, that Lesbian caress! . . . Nor twine like ivy round my feet, uttering that awful moan for blighted joys! . . .

Witold, O Witold! behold, I return to you! O sleep, O life! Yes, I return. . . .

I have written the following short note to Witold to-day:

"If you wish, you may come. J. D."

It breathed the spite—the unavailing and very plebeian spite—of my humiliation. I fully recognized this: and yet I chose to send the note, thus styled.

I expected that he would come like a conqueror, triumphant and self-assured; and thinking so, I for the time being ceased to love him at all.

As it happened, he has belied my expectations.

On my return from the office, I found him already here. He was quite childishly delighted, and for a long while I could not free myself from his rapturous embrace.

"Janka, Janka! how cruel, how cruel you have been!" he cried out in broken words amongst his kisses. "You are a monster of barbarity! And of stubbornness too! For you know so well how much I love you! . . . You should have had trust in me, as I have trust in you. . . . Have I ever given you any cause for mistrust? I hide nothing from you, nothing whatsoever! . . . Oh, my dearest, my only one, my darling! . . . I know that you will be mine one day—mine! It must be so. . . . Could I ever have exposed myself to the danger of losing your love? Think of that. Think how different you are from all other women. . . . I know you could never have forgiven me, if . . ."

So handsome, so kindly, so affectionate! I knew how intensely I loved him. And then, in the secret depths of my heart of hearts, I was aware that I could forgive him anything in the world.

Yet I said: "My love for you would then instantly turn to hate, as it did for the last few days. . . ."

He feigned to be horribly frightened. We were both of us in ecstasies of joy.

Long, long, did we speak together of our love. We should love each other forever and forever: and with what intensity! . . . Only we were to have more of mutual trust, and to be more tolerant one for the other: there would be no more of those former bickerings which had been so painful to both of us.

Closer and closer we drew. Hallucinated with rapture, I was almost out of my mind. The air around me grew rosy, and the walls had a purple glow, and the lamp was burning—how can I express it? Black, quite black! Bending down his head, he fixed his eyes on me.

"Janka!" he said, with low but clear-cut articulation; "Janka!" His voice was changed; it was strangled and seething with emotion. There was in it just a touch of surprise—surprise at the victory which he now foresaw.

I was startled, and a shiver ran through me.
A noise as of a whirlwind murmured confus-
edly in my ears; my throat was filled with a
hot suffocating fragrance, and I felt as if the
air I breathed had grown solid and came in
morsels.

"Janka, Janka," he whispered again, as if
struggling with his deep perturbation; for he
was greatly moved.

In a sort of hypnotic trance, I stared hard
into his dimly glistening eyes. I kissed his
mouth. . . . All my soul, with all its faculties,
transported from the infinitely distant con-
fines of the world of thought, was concentrated and poured out in that one kiss of mine!

Ah! I cannot understand what it was that at
such a moment held me back, since I and all
that was mine had now been transformed and
had passed into one desire alone. It was no
longer thirst, it was hunger—raging, ravenous
hunger. I clung to him with all my might,
and whispered and stammered a string of
broken incoherent words; and, in a delirium
of mingled agony and bliss, I sighed under
my breath:

"Oh, my only one; oh, my own!"

And afterwards—afterwards, when he had

left my side, ungratified and disappointed, as
he ever had been—then, with a burst of heart-
rending tears, I threw myself down upon the
floor near the door which had just closed on
him, and listened to the sound of his footsteps,
and murmured imploringly:

"Oh, come—come—come back! I am
yours!"

But had he come back—I knew it well—I
should have resisted then, as always.

And perhaps it is true to say that such a
thirst as mine was cannot possibly be quenched
by any delight on earth!

All is once more as it was of old. I am
much in love, happy (to some extent), and
slightly sarcastic ·about things in general.
Witold comes daily; he is good and tender to
me beyond words.

Sometimes our conversation flags. Then
we read together—novels and poems only; for
Witold, scientific literature is non-existent. A
volume of Owinski's poems, just published,
has given us many a pleasant hour.

She is right, Idalia: I had taken all things
—and that also—too much in earnest. At

present, I am trying to live more practically
than I ever did.

Of the present situation, nothing can come
—neither marriage nor anything else. So, as
I reckon, it may last at the most one year
more. I have to be prepared for that, and let
the parting come by degrees and as easily as
possible; so I am looking beforehand for some
rock or other to which I may cling when
wrecked. Now and then, when I think of my
ideals once cherished in the past, the notion
still comes to me (though rarely) of a love
both *deep* and *wise*.

Better seek something far other than love—
an "aim in life"—some idea—asceticism—
even such as a nunnery can provide! *"Dans la
bête assouvie un ange se réveille!"* Yes, but
—is it *"assouvie"*? Well, I am rather tired,
not only of love, but of the whole atmosphere
I am living in.

In truth, disdain of all things is best of all.
Yet again, disdain itself would be one of the
things to be disdained!

I am curiously entangled at present, and can
scarcely recognize myself as "Her of the Ice-
Plains." In this continual struggle with myself, my strength has been exhausted.

Ah, yes; another incident. Czolhanski has proposed to me in the most naïve fashion imaginable. Although I am a woman of "advanced" ideas (and they say such a one hardly can make a good wife), still he is not alarmed; he trusts in me! Besides, he could not live with any woman unable to understand him. . . . Also, he gets two hundred roubles a month, which, together with my office salary, . . . And so on.

I have refused him categorically, hopelessly, irrevocably. And—which is much more strange—I have done so without the shadow of a smile.

When I am very weary and out of sorts, I go and call up Wiazewski. There are people who resemble those ships which were formerly used by slave traders to convey their human freight: these had a double hold. And Wiazewski is one of such men.

He allows any one to overhaul his soul on the asking, freely and frankly. Only he does not like them, when they come to the hold, to knock too hard: the hollow sound underneath would betray his secret. Beneath the false bottom, there is a dark den into which he smuggles those he has enslaved to his will, never to go out free into the world again. The knowledge of this would spoil his reputation in society as an estimable man.

"Do you know, Stephen, you look like a man who has a bit of a tragedy upon his conscience, and is concealing it."

He laughed. "Since when has Janka begun to grow romantic?"

"Since I fell in love, of course!"

"You!!" Astounded, he stared at me.

"My dear friend, what can there be to surprise you in that?"

"I really . . . no, really I do not know. I was only taken aback. Certainly, on your side, it is but a natural thing. Don't you see? I had grown so accustomed to look on you as belonging to a third sex."

"There now, how unjust you have been! I on my own part have always looked on you as a man."

"But come, tell me with whom you are in love, and whether your bliss is all that fancy painted it."

I shrugged my shoulders.

"Bliss! It is you who are romantic now,

Stephen. At the best, I am not bored. And the less bliss I have, the less bored I am!"

"Then you are not bored?"

"Oh, I am—very much so at times. At such moments, I come and call on you. I have learned to cherish our disinterested friendship ever more and more."

He moved as if annoyed a little; then he lit a cigarette.

"Whom?"

"I don't understand."

"Whom do you love?"

"Oh, an ideal according to your own taste. *A bon entendeur salut.*" Note: All the better if you have caught my meaning.

"Won't you tell me?"

"No, I won't. Guess, if you want to know."

"A fool?"

"To some extent, yes."

"Handsome?"

"Too much so by far."

"Wealthy?"

"Indifferently."

"It is—it is Imszanski! *Et tu, Janka!*" he exclaimed, looking into my face with a curious expression.

I knew what question was implied by his look, and slowly shook my head.

He breathed more freely.

"And yet I should never have imagined..."

"How's that? I have only been practising your own theory of love."

"Ye—es, but . . ."

"Well, but what?"

"This is quite another thing. Of primitive elemental simplicity he has nothing at all."

"It is true. In that point, and in that point only, has my practice departed from your theory. But I think good art is not unfrequently preferable to problematical simplicity."

"Yes, no doubt. And, moreover . . ."

"Pray continue."

"I myself have ended by abandoning that theory of mine. My experience with Helena exploded it definitely. I have radically changed my attitude; now I am without any conviction at all on the subject."

"But I imagined that the fallen edifice of your theory was to be restored by the aid of kitchen-maids."

"Vain hopes! They have proved impracticable, even to myself. My experiments in that quarter only completed the ruin of the theory."

"Well, then, what are you going to do about it?"

"I am seeking love."

"Oh, dear! *Et tu!* And it was to you I came on purpose to get a rest from it. There must be some fatality about all this—the atmosphere is vitiated everywhere. . . . Stephen, have mercy, have mercy!"

He smiled compassionately.

"So soon as that? Janka, how soon you get tired!"

We went to a *café,* where we saw Gina sitting along with Radlowski at one of the tables. There were none vacant, so we joined them at theirs, and I introduced the men to each other. Wiazewski objects to artists; but he must have been pleased with this one, whose exterior is that of a typical "gentleman." I was in exceedingly good spirits, and set about flirting with the painter. He was now much changed from what he was when I saw him last. His eyes are not bright any more, and he looks a good deal older. We fell to talking upon speculative subjects, and I strove to be original and sparkling. Radlowski's eyes were fixed steadfastly on my face all the while.

"Well, I see you are far more of a woman than I had ever thought you."

My answer to these words of Stephen's was only a look, but a look of triumph. At last it had come—this, the hardest of all victories to win! . . . Unfortunately, it came too late. . . .

"In a few years," he added, "when all your faculties are duly balanced, you will be an exceptional being. Perhaps a model 'Woman of the Future.'"

"Oh, anything but that. I take no interest except in what goes on within me. If I am at all elated, it is not on account of what is there, but of the fact that these forces are incessantly in conflict with my will. I am proud of my imperfections which turn to perfections, of my ideas which treat one another with mutual contempt, of my instincts, so strongly opposed to my logic; of my atavistic tendencies, which it is a finer and more momentous work to unearth and to note down than to put into practice. I am proud of the eternal Becoming, teeming with riches, dazzling with the wildest hues, deafening with harsh discordancies, rushing on, moving hither and thither, turning in spiral ascension, or even spinning round. Yes, I am proud that this Becoming still goes on. I prefer a hundred times the 'Transitional Woman' to the 'Woman of the Future': for she who is transitional promises ever so much more than the other, when perfect, can fulfil.

"Neither you," I said, turning to Gina, "with your quasi-Pantheistic theory of love; nor Madame Wildenhoff, with her volatile and almost man-like eroticism; nor Idalia, nor Martha—none of you is, any more than I am, a woman of the future; you are full of exaggerated theories, of crotchets, of false notions, of atavistic trends and extreme views. Yet I prefer you to that free and happy woman of our dreams, in whom desire, conscious and in perfect equilibrium, will not, however intense it may be, ·trespass beyond the limits of its possibility to be satisfied. Yes! You I prefer to the most perfect of standards, to the very best of patterns, to the wisest and most consistent of—Philistines!"

Gina said gloomily:

"Then what is it all for—this ghastly struggle, this agony of Becoming?"

"For the glory of the last specimens of our

species. We are tending towards this goal:
that the abstract type of Woman may perish
as soon as it is realized, even as the abstract
type of Man perished also. Having attained
that level, we shall, together with Man, begin
to evolve in the wider sphere of our common
humanity. The struggle and the war of the
elements which make up our nature will still
continue in a new Becoming, but no longer in
the narrow space of womanhood, which leaves
us too little room to breathe."

"All the same," said Stephen, in conclusion,
"our descendants will envy us very, very much,
since we live in the days of the Last Woman."

"Let us hope that the present period may
endure for some time; say, until the gorilla
is extinct."

Stephen's feeling of mediæval worship for
woman was shocked at my words: "Women
and gorillas named together!" he sighed.

Whilst we were going home, after taking
leave of Gina and Radlowski, he said, hesi-
tatingly and in some confusion:

"Janka, do not make a pastime of that
Imszanski any more: he is not worth playing
with."

"Well said, but? . . ."

"Hear me out, Janka. Till the present moment, I was not aware that I loved you and you alone. . . . May I hope, or is it quite out of the question?"

"Good God, Stephen! pray don't think of proposing! I got a proposal only the other day. There must be something in the air—infection—the approach of spring! At any rate, I am not in a consenting mood now; so let me be."

I laughed, but was in reality very much upset.

When last together, Gina asked me to come over to her apartments, as she wanted me to read something she had.

It was almost gayly that she welcomed me in. Her eyes had lost their customary look of apathy, and shone with a strange fire.

"Owinski is going to be married this very week," she remarked, as if stating a fact which did not concern her. "Have you read his poems?"

"I have; Witold and I read them together."

"One of his poems had been dedicated to me; I know, for I myself saw it in proof—a proof that I myself corrected. And now the dedication has been removed from the title. When he received the revised proof, he probably crossed it off."

She then took two closely written sheets of letter-paper out of a drawer.

"A letter from her!" she explained.

"To you!"

"Yes. Just read it."

It ran thus:

"I have long been wishing to write to you, Madame; and if I have not made up my mind till now, this was neither from any want of courage on my part, nor any misplaced sense of delicacy, which would in this case be not only exaggerated, but groundless. It simply proceeded from the fact that, as I think the greatest alleviation of sorrow to consist in the possibility of hating some one on account of it, I did not like to deprive you of the object of your hate. For I am of opinion that, as soon as you have read this, you will not think me your enemy any more.

"If I write now, it is because I believe that, in lieu of such consolation, I am able to afford you another; and I do so without the knowledge of my *fiancé*, for I have my doubts whether it would be pleasant to him or the reverse; and besides, I do not consider him as the sole means by which we might come to understand each other.

"The evening on which we were both under the same roof has remained with me as a painful memory. Not because I then felt at all to blame on your account. As I had been aware from the beginning that O. was affianced, I played no active part in the matter to attract him. Any other woman might have been in my place, and done just the same, so far as you were concerned. O. was at that time in want of a figure upon his life chessboard, such as is called a formally affianced wife; so we met and encountered each other by mere chance—a happening without logical relevance to anything. Nor was it because I felt for you what is called pity. My mind would never consent to abase you by venturing to entertain such a feeling; and I think, too, that I am an object of pity not less than yourself. No; the meeting was painful to me only for the following reason; I myself, looking on things as an outsider, cannot help having a fellow-feeling for all who have been worsted; so that I experienced self-dislike. It was

painful, because I was present to your mind as
a stranger, a successful rival, nothing but the
fiancée of your *fiancé,* a hostile, unknown She:
not a woman, drawn close to you by your and
my sense of our hard fate. It was painful to
me to sit so far apart from you, to be unable
to approach you and look into your thought-
ful eyes with eyes that were not less thought-
ful, and kindly too, and talk to you about
many a subject far more important than the
law which thrusts us apart: the law, known
from time immemorial, that love is not everlasting, and that it needs variety.

"To write of my friendly feeling towards
you would certainly seem somewhat paradox-
ical. I will therefore say no more than this;
I deeply and sincerely esteem you, as one after
my own heart, as a New Woman, a woman
conscious of her own value and of her rights;
I appreciate you also for your subtlety of emotion, and your original artistic talent. And
then, besides, I have a certain debt of gratitude
which is due to you personally, and owing to
the fact that O. has for several years been
pretty faithful to you; and thus the list of his
transitory amours which distress me so is considerably shorter than it would otherwise have

been. I bear you no grudge, no, not even
when O. (for my delectation!) goes back into
the past, and tells me all about his former love
for you.

"I trust you feel no longer any instinctive
dislike or aversion for me; do you? And now
I will, in return for what you have to suffer,
give you the information that you have indeed
but very little reason to envy my lot. Like
you, I am one of those unhappy beings who
must needs suffer, whatever their circumstances may be, because life is too brutally in-
exorable, and we—we whose nerves are laid
bare—cannot walk through life without suffering. Then, examining the question quite
objectively, may we not unhesitatingly assert
that it is preferable to endure suffering for a
positive loss, whilst we enjoy the memory of
past happiness (or at least the illusion that
such happiness would have been possible, had
circumstances and environment been different), rather than to endure it at that one period
of our lives when we ought not to suffer at all?
than to experience such distress as excludes
the possibility that we may so much as dream
of ever being happy? Is not misery at its
height in the very springtime of life, when

the faculty of possible enjoyment is most developed? In this indeed, the lot of our *fiancé* is always and invariably an enviable one. I am not happy, and I doubt whether you have ever known happiness. A strange being he is, forever plucking flowers and smiling in the sunshine, yet unceasingly, and often unwittingly, marking his road through life by the pain he gives to others, and by the tears, so vain and so unworthy of us, which he makes us shed.

"So I am not writing to you in order that I may enjoy my honeymoon without remorse, for—as I say once more—I do not consider that I have done you any wrong. I only want you to know me just as I am, and not to look upon me as a stranger or a foe. I am not given to sentiment, and do not fear the hatred of people: on the contrary, I rather like it; but I do not wish *you* to hate me. What a sad thing it would be, if a poet could succeed in separating two intelligent and agreeable women from each other for ever!

"I kiss you, and with the warmest affection. . . ."

"A sweet creature she is!" I remarked, and looked at Gina.

She was looking depressed, and much older. Her eyes were bedimmed, and wandering helplessly from piece to piece of furniture, from wall to wall.

"And she does not even feel any love for him! A cold-hearted being, made for nothing but to chop logic! And he—for her, for her . . . ! Ah, the cruel wrong! Why has this come to me?"

She put her hands up to her head and sobbed aloud. . . .

Suddenly she snatched the letter from me, and crumpled it up, and tore it all to pieces with angry fingers.

"How I hate, oh, how I hate that woman!"

I brought her a glass of water to calm her nerves, thinking all the time how much, in this, her unjust outburst of fury, she was preferable to the other—the magnanimous, serene, lofty-minded New Woman.

Smilowicz, of all men in the world! was awaiting me outside the office to-day.

Time, I thought, had for an instant run backward; and the Past, so terribly gone and forgotten, was before me.

"What! You!" I exclaimed; "you, back

from Siberia? How long have you been here?
. . . I had not been told——"

"The manifesto: an amnesty . . . Five
years. Yes, five have passed by. I arrived
last week, and have seen nobody but Obojanski. He did not even know your address!
Was that nice of you? . . . Oh, how greatly
you have changed! . . . No, I did not expect
such backsliding on your part . . . I have
heard many things said . . ."

"And what about yourself?"

I saw that his plain face, which was now
adorned with a thin stubbly beard, was much
emaciated. His former careless smile was
now quite gone, and his features were darkened and bronzed like a peasant's.

"I?" He smiled, but with his lips only, that
were always drawn: once with suffering, now
with having suffered. "I? You never would
guess. I married down there; yes, I married
a fellow-exile. And we have a son."

"But what of your health? And what are
you going to do in Warsaw?"

"Something or other." He raised his hand,
palm down, then let it drop limply. "At present I am more or less amongst the unemployed.

Besides, I am consumptive. . . . On the whole, prospects not very brilliant."

I asked him to come to my lodgings.

He looked uneasy. "Are you living with—
them?" he asked.

"No; now no longer."

"Ah, that's very good. . . . Professor Obojanski told me fearful things about you, and they grieved me. He must have been exaggerating: he bears you a deep grudge for having broken with him so. For he appreciates you very highly indeed. He counts your having thrown yourself away like that as the greatest disappointment he ever had in his life."

So we went down the road, chatting about old times. He informed me that Roslawski had gone off on some Polar expedition. I used to call him the "Autocrat of the Iceplains": it seems that he belongs to them at any rate.

"But now," Smilowicz blurted out, rather bashfully, "hadn't you better come and see us? I have told Sophy (my wife) all about you; she would like to make your acquaintance, and does not know anybody in Warsaw. And you will see Andy, my little boy!"

I of course agreed.

Mme. Smilowicz received us in a tiny room —bachelor's lodgings on the fourth floor— amongst a confused medley of boxes and mattresses and lumber of various kinds. She began by asking us to speak low, not to disturb Andy, who was then asleep: then she showed him to me: a one-year-old baby, asleep in a cradle. It had a tilted Mongolian nose, the result, no doubt, of the mother's having so often seen the type.

I paid it several compliments, of the What-a-fine-baby sort, and had not the least fear of being suspected of irony.

For the rest, Mme. Smilowicz has not the appearance of a "youthful mother"; she is a thin black-avised little woman in a dark gown, with a double eye-glass on her nose.

She poured some spirits of wine into the little pan for heating the kettle, and while it was burning itself out, she said, very low:

"My dear Madame, people say that women are weaker than men. But they do not in the least take into account all the strength that we expend over the children; just as if it were uselessly wasted! But furthermore, and setting this aside, let any one of them try to go through what I have undergone. With a child one year old, my dear Madame! in that bleak ice-bound land! and then, on our way home, having to do everything, my husband in wretched health. . . . And here again, look you! notwithstanding all this work on my hands, I have managed to translate thus much: and now we shall be able to sell it somewhere. Joseph dear, have you been able to see the publisher to-day?"

She pointed to a heap of papers, written in a fine female hand. Her husband smiled at me proudly.

As soon as the spirits were burnt out, Mme. Smilowicz worked the piston with swift strokes, pumping up a stream of gas, while her husband held a match to light it as it issued forth. A loud droning sound was heard, and a slight smell of naphtha was discernible.

"Won't the noise wake little Andy?" I queried, with sham solicitude.

"No, no, he is accustomed to it now."

We took tea, discussing abstract topics the while. I had not read any of the books which they mentioned; and I found this a hard thing to acknowledge. I had the impression of being spirited away on to some other planet, and felt all the time out of countenance and like an intruder. Also, my new dress was in such glaring and unpleasant contrast with its environment here: and I had it borne in upon me that my life, too, was in the same contrast.

After the machine had been put out and droned no more, there was heard a noise of children from beyond the partition wall: a hubbub as of many voices, now and then interrupted by the thin sound of a piercing female voice. On the fourth floor, a lot of youngsters were making merry.

"Do you hear that, Madame? And it is just the same, every day almost. They are dreadfully in the way of my work. Why are the walls made so thin?"

I was amazed, and could not help rather envying her; the contrast between us was so very glaring, and yet she had not even remarked it! She was thinking only of this annoyance; made no comparison, drew no parallel whatever!

Andy in his cradle now set up a loud and lusty wailing.

She jumped up from the table, jostling me in her haste, and rocked the child to sleep again, crooning low an inarticulate lullaby, tuneless, wordless, and not unlike that broken croaking which frogs utter. And again and again she would say:

"Little son of mine, my only one, my beautiful one!"

And then, sitting down to tea again, she spoke in a most interesting way about one of the books she had recently translated. It was from the English—essays on Economics.

"Joseph encourages me to write something as well; but for that one must have one's mind more at ease."

Then, with a tender look that she cast on her husband:

"I think," she said, "that Joseph will soon be better in our climate; when he was sent away from Poland, he was in perfect health. Do you remember how he looked in those days?"

"Certainly I do; very well indeed."

And I proceeded to tell her of the expeditions we both used to make to Obojanski's.

"But," I observed, "you have worked a miracle; he was always absolutely insensible to the charms of womankind." This I said out of kindness, fearing lest I might otherwise give occasion to thoughts of jealousy and suspicion.

I soon felt, however, that such delicacy was out of place and lost upon her; she was impervious to any fancies of that kind.

"When at the High School," she told me, "I made it my purpose in life to reconcile my duties toward society with those that I owed to myself. People who are against women's emancipation say that no woman can at the same time go in for book-learning and be a good wife and mother. That is their strongest argument. But, if only women themselves would recognize that this is possible, and that everything can be made to agree! I myself, my dear Madame, finished my course of Sociology in Brussels, where I even published a short paper in French. Since then I have followed the onward march of science, so as to be always up-to-date: I am reading continually, and am occupied in translating at present. . . . Sometimes, too, I am able to help Joseph with facts and information. And now I ask you, my dear Madame, could the most stolid *bourgeoise,* if placed in my circumstances, give herself more to her child than I do! Consider, I have no nursemaid, nor any of the aids which those much belauded 'good mothers' enjoy. I suckle the baby myself, I tidy the room, I do the cooking, the porteress brings me provisions from the market, and that is all. Oh, how I wish some of those keen-witted gentlemen could come here and see!"

"Yes," Smilowicz put in here, "if a working woman is out of doors all day long, leaving her children uncared for, that is in order and reasonable and right! But let a woman consecrate a few hours to her studies in the evening, they will say this is emancipation, and incompatible with her duties as a mother."

I could see how gratified she was to hear this.

"I am only sorry for those who do not know what exceeding happiness is to be found in marriage, if there is but mutual understanding and sympathy." And she glanced at her husband with extreme tenderness.

Meanwhile, there was a continual noise on the other side of the partition, and there came a curiously disturbing sound of women's voices, cackling with a sort of scandalized laughter—something between giggling and sobbing.

Smilowicz's attention was drawn off by it.

"What beasts they are!" he said at last, to relieve his feelings.

"They are not malicious, but unhappy," she said. "For them too, I feel sorry."

Smilowicz made no reply. Presently he was trying to persuade me to go over and see Obojanski one of these days.

"Always plunged in those books of his— overhead and ears in them—indifferent to everything else that goes on throughout the wide world. His study seems to me now such a haven as one might dream for. . . . Yes, let us go one day and visit him, Miss Janina."

Really, no bad notion, that. As to Smilowicz's surroundings, they do not agree with me. Since I have got rid of all such associations, I do not care to return to them. And then, that woman! Willingly would I throw her out of the window to the Idealistic dreamer of the noble New Woman, equal to Man; and I should cry *Ecce femina!* Like Diogenes throwing the plucked cock to Plato.

Yes; for the vision of the Idealist is realized —thus!

But Obojanski, the venerable, grey-bearded Master, with his mien of a Greek sage; and his never-ending, shallow sophistries and cheap disputes upon matters of the highest import; and even his many volumes of monographs on insects—all this has something that to me is singularly attracting!

To-day, tenderness and mutual vows once more. . . . Ay, we shall love, love, love each other till . . .

"Listen, Witold; for how long are we to be in love so?" I asked; a question I myself had not expected to put.

"Forever," he answered with absolute assurance.

"And how long is this 'forever' to last?"

"Ah, well—of course—as long as we live. Do you believe in love beyond the grave?"

"Decidedly not!"

"Then, until death. And as I shall surely be the first to drop off, I shall have the best of it." And he bowed as a courtier in Versailles, two centuries ago.

I concentrated my thoughts for a time. Behold me, sitting, clad in the raiments of ancient Greece, upon a bench of stone, my bare and shapely elbow resting on a balustrade. . . . Bending over the marble barrier, I look down, coldly, scrutinizingly, into the depths beyond—the depths of my soul. And behold, it is an abyss more than of infinite depth.—Alas! my ponderings, imaged thus, tell me but that in such an attitude. and thus arrayed, I look very handsome!

The sun is glaring high in heaven. Floating on the bright sea-waves is a light bark, with the prow shaped like a swan's neck; and Witold is sitting in the bark. He smiles as he floats so lightly—floats on the sea of life. And I—I remain aimlessly gazing into those depths of my own being. . . .

"Witold, you know that all this sort of thing must, sooner or later, come to an end?"

"How should I know that?"

"Not by experience?"

"Ah! Janka, my dearest, how often have I entreated you!" Then, in a gayer tone: "I am not an experimentalist in any sense of the word. And it is thus that I know to-day just as much as I did yesterday; and I cling to my illusions as I did of old times."

"But why will you never consider this question with your eyes open and face to face? Why are you for ever afraid of it? Why must the dreadful burden of seeing things clearly always be borne by me? Oh, Witold!"

He did not answer me, but walked nervously up and down the apartment. Then, coming to a stop at a small table, with his face turned away from me, he lit a cigarette.

A short silence followed. Then I went on.

"It's not that I want anyone to lean upon. Understand me. I am not in need of any sustaining or protecting power. I only wish for some power able to counterbalance my own. I want to be helped by strength equivalent to that which I myself put forth: I would only have an equal weight in each scale. . . . Oh, if you but knew how terrified I am, when my scale, becoming heavier, sinks down, down, into the very lowest depths of my sad unfathomable pride!"

Here I paused for a time, awaiting some reply.

Unexpectedly, he began to speak, quietly, in smooth tones, and without looking in my direction.

"Let me tell you, Janka—I never yet spoke to you about this, but to-day I must: it weighs upon me too heavily, too insupportably. Straightforward I am, it may be, but I am not a man who enjoys telling the truth; I simply don't like it. Well, there's one point . . ."

He broke off, to continue presently in yet smoother tones.

"There's one point—I must tell you, my dearest love, that you make me suffer extreme tortures. Yes, you do. You sometimes torture me to such an extent that I lose all self-command, all patience. . . . I am in torments, to put it plainly—I beseech you, believe what I am saying now. I cannot break myself in to accept your theories. I am unable; besides, I will not. . . . You make no sacrifice, you. Have you ever given anything up for my sake? No. If not, you have no right to lay down conditions. You must take me as I am; try to understand me and to adapt yourself to me, rather than me to yourself. Remember, I have no sympathy whatever with high-flown sentiments; I cannot walk on stilts. I cannot, no, I cannot! All that is such a trial to me that I am often longing to get away—away—as far as I possibly can go! And so I concoct untruths, invent mythical shooting and supper-parties, and go to imaginary meetings—simply because I have to breathe now and then. You can see that I am at present speaking the truth! Not that I do not love you! Oh, no! who is it—if I did not love you so deeply, so intensely as I do—who is it that could make me bear this even for one instant? . . . Truly, you have not the slightest idea to what lengths of despotism your strong individuality drives you. Your demands on me are endless, Janka; you put me in fetters, with your exactions, and those tastes of yours that I have to follow. Have I ever, in anything whatever, interfered with you? No; never have I brought forward the slightest claim to anything; nay, I have preferred that you should feel yourself in some respect to be in arrears with me, for I reverence the liberty of others. Why can you not have the same toleration for me? . . . And then, for the life of me, I cannot make out why you are, all of you, of such jealous dispositions; nor why you all go on everlastingly philosophizing in that way!"

His outbreak having exhausted him, he sat down on an arm-chair at some distance from me, and proceeded to light another cigarette.

For many minutes, I was dumbstruck, trying to dig my way out of the ruins of that building which had fallen upon me so suddenly and in a way so unforeseen. Who would have expected this from this page of mine, with his sweet, tawny eye-lashes.

At first, I was unable to realize it.

"But I see, Witold, that you have not the least love for me—that is, for what is most essential in me; I have at last found it out."

I mused awhile.

"And then, besides, what you say is untrue. Recall which of us two revels more in high-flown, naïve, silly, maudlin sentiment! Who was it was always dreaming of an ideal 'brotherhood of souls,' instead of regarding love in the ordinary way? It was I who cannot bear what is high-flown; I, who always had to bring you down from your stilts."

Witold was looking out of the window. There was in his bearing aristocratic boredom and lassitude, plainly expressed.

"Ah, Janka," he said, this time in a tone of supreme indifference, "that, too, is on your part all theory. Of this you only make use, that you may struggle against the high-flown sentimentality which you feel within you, though you disown it, and deny its existence. And the eternal conflict with yourself in which you are plunged, and your empty theories, with their unconscious hypocrisy—these are the best proof of what I say, and the most high-flown sentimentality of all. . . . Only you delude yourself. . . . You are just as other women are, capable of infinite self-devotion and sacrifice. Hear me still. If I were now to love you no longer, to go away from you and forget you (men forget so very readily), you would be longing for me, and in anguish, like any other woman in the same situation, and in spite of all your 'positive' theories; you would be miserable, as you were during the last two weeks when we were parted; and you would again write first to me. And should I not come in answer to it—as I had a great mind not to come, nothwithstanding my 'idealistic' way of looking at love— why then, you would write again and again, even to the tenth time! Don't say you would not; I know you well. Oh, how well I know women! I'll tell you what: I am still more certain that you love me and will be faithful than I was in Martha's case, for all you say about paying me in my own coin, if I were false. Martha could forget herself for my sake; you never could. A bundle of theories, of sentimental scepticism, of self-assurance: that's what you are! A poor frightened bird always popping its head under its wing!"

I felt quite broken. There was an immense

and awful void in my heart. I had the odd
delusion—or had his words suggested the
feeling?—that I really experienced the weakness of which he spoke, and was unable to escape from his hands. Thereupon, I began to
cry.

"I don't—I don't believe—that you ever
loved me!"

In an instant he had changed his manner,
and become kind and gentle as he had always
been before. He came to my side, with
caresses and words of comfort; even a little
friendly banter.

"Alas!" I groaned; "why did you never tell
me about this before?"

"Because I was quite sure that you would
burst out crying, as you are doing at present,
you naughty child!"

At those words, directly and on the spur
of the moment, there fell upon me a sense of
strong distaste. Back to my memory came
in swarms all sorts of seeming trifles, which,
together with many a minute detail of our
past, made proof demonstrative and irrefut-
able . . . of what he was.

"And you were quite sure, Witold, of
something else into the bargain!"

"What was that, Janka?"

With downcast eyes I answered, smiling:
"That I should never love you any more."

I had spoken with absolute candour and
certitude. I knew this to be a necessity of life
to me; and I wiped my last tears away—

"Bah! give over, little girl. Do you not
see this too is silly sentiment? You yourself
don't believe what you say." He still spoke
as in tones of tranquil persuasion; but I could
see disquietude looking out of his eyes.

I smiled at him once more, saying:
"Whether I believe or not, matters little.
What matters is that you certainly do!"

He turned a trifle pale, and felt nervously
for his cigarette-case. "Give over!" he cried
out roughly, on a sudden, and again came
towards me.

I rose, quivering all over with excitement,
but managed to say, calmly enough:

"I should not like to part from you too
tragically. And since I have had enough of
love in general, and enough of your person
especially, I am afraid I must ask you to have
the goodness to withdraw now. Let us
shake hands on parting. Go."

He came forwards, with knit gloomy

brows, and looks which betrayed the storm that raged within him. I stepped backwards. He stood for an instant struggling with himself, and I fully expected he would rush at me.

But his breeding prevailed. He made a courtly bow, kissed my hand and retired.

I stood where I was, with head bent forward. . . . That page, with his dear tawny eye-lashes—with his soft sad eyes—with his lips, of the odour of faded roses—he that once had been mine!

"All the same," I whispered to myself, "the thing is done at last!"

To-day I feel I have crossed the Rubicon, and am standing on the farther shore, not very sure whether things are better with me now. And yet, I should not wish to go back again.

I have this morning received several nosegays.

Flowers to embellish the funeral repast! Flowers on the coffin of one gone forever!

But that is nothing. No, nothing, I swear! Often and often the monument over a sepulchre may turn into a gate that leads to a new life.

Smilowicz has come to see me.

He, too, is mentally depressed at times: which I should never have suspected.

He edged himself into the very arm-chair in which Witold had been seated last evening. For some time he was silent; and then: "There are days," he said, "when I think myself an idiot for having wasted my life over a mere shadow. Oh, how I envy you!"

"Why, is your life wasted?" I cried in amazement.

"You have been at our lodgings—and you have seen." . . .

"Well?"

"You have seen all!"

"But your wife is a happy woman," I said, trying to take the optimistic side of things; though all the time I was saying to myself (and I really don't know why): "How is love possible between those two?"

"My wife may be so," he said, slowly. "Sometimes I cannot."

"They say it is a great thing to have children. Even if you do not attain the goal you aim at, there always remains something of you."

My remark elicited no reply from him. I

could see painful and bitter thoughts flit over his thin face, as he looked round the room.

"You have no end of flowers!" he murmured.

"These are all *flowers of farewell*. These at least you need not envy me."

His face darkened.

"You know how ill I am. That is what makes me so hateful. Not that I regret life, but that I have nothing in life to regret losing."

I did not answer.

"To know for sure that death is at hand gives you quite another outlook upon life. An extraordinary attachment to things positive springs up, together with an intense hate for abstractions. Each renunciation, each victory over self, is to you like a fresh nail in your coffin."

"But you surely love your wife?" I asked him, after a pause.

"I do."

"And your son, too?"

He gave a nod.

"Well, then . . ." I tried to draw some comforting inference, but unsuccessfully.

"Well, then . . ." I repeated once more, and once more relapsed into helpless silence.

"Ah, how kind you are!" he said in a low voice, and looked at me for some time with a grateful expression. "And how beautiful besides!" he added unexpectedly.

I felt startled: mere instinct on my part, for I had no reason to fear. He glanced away from me, and turned his attention to some orchids that stood close to him, stroking them with his bony hand.

"When I ask myself now for what reason I did what I did, I can find no answer to my question. Such flowers as these; I have gone through life, always trampling upon them; why? Why should Obojanski cut them to pieces, that he may, in them and from them, hit upon some new abstraction or other—their genus, their species, their variety? Why do you call them *flowers of farewell?* Oh, now that I know how terrible the way of self-denial and virtue is, I should this day like to lie on a bed of flowers such as these."

"I can answer to your question: You trampled the flowers, because you were a strong man."

"Is love of life a weakness then?" He fell a-thinking.

"Perhaps it is. Perhaps I care for life for the same reason that made Voltaire confess before he died: vital energy giving way. And after all, life!"

Here I set to explain to him at great length that life is in reality an evil, and not worth regretting when it goes from us, that in its track it leaves a bitterness still greater than the bitterness of self-denial and self-control, and evokes a yet stronger reaction. . . .

To that he said: "Yes, the reaction which life brings is directed against life, and makes it easier to die. All the better."

"It is well," he added. "It is not after all life itself that I wish for. I wish only to be convinced—convinced by experience that life is an evil thing. This is all that I would have."

When he left me, I presented him with a great many flowers, begging him, as a pretext, to carry them to his wife from me.

Looking out of the window, I saw him going his way, clad in a fur, notwithstanding the mildness of the weather, and pressing my flowers to his heart.

In the evening, I sent to Wiazewski, asking him to step in. I thought he would be some consolation to me; but though he made visible endeavours to show good humour, he had none. I therefore proposed we should take a walk.

It was a splendid night, fine and breezy, and steeped in the sweet, drowsy, dizzying perfume of coming spring. The lamplights twinkled away, far into the distance, like innumerable strings of diamonds; the streets were deserted, but brightly lit. The white moon was now and then visible above the irregular line of the housetops. All was picturesquely calm and cold—a condition that I especially like.

Our way led us down a great thoroughfare, along which a few belated carriages were passing.

Stephen was jesting; but it went against the grain. He was telling me about the tragical fate of some disappointed suitor.

Just in front of us, at the very corner of the street, and opposite the doorway of a large hotel, a brilliantly elegant equipage, coming at full speed, suddenly pulled up.

A servant ran to open the carriage-door.

Witold jumped out nimbly, and helped a woman to descend.

Springing lightly from the step, and walking by his side at a rapid pace, magnificent in billowy furbelows and lace, and spreading around her an atmosphere of dainty odours, Iseult Lermeaux went in.

Witold's eye caught mine at the very moment when, helping her out of the carriage, he was about to take her arm. In the glare of the electric lamps, I saw him turn deadly pale. He bowed instinctively; his arms dropped to his side: he was at a loss what to do. Wiazewski's presence embarrassed him, and he stood like one transfixed. She turned round and also glanced at us.

And thus they disappeared as we walked down the long bright vista of the street, and we saw them no more. "No laggard, that man!" I thought. "The very next day!"

"As I don't wish you to feel sorry for me, Stephen, I will inform you that I have already broken with that gentleman; so that his doings do not concern me in the least now."

At my words, Wiazewski slackened his pace.

"Why, in that case, Janka . . ." he began.

"Pray, Stephen, don't. I begged you once before——"

He said nothing further then, and walked on for a considerable time with head bent down; finally, he said to me in an undertone:

"May we not think of marriage, merely as a bond of friendship?"

"No, no! . . . Can you not see that a wife never has the disinterestedness of a friend? How can she be at one with her husband in everything? In many cases, she would be wronging herself. For instance, what interests me most in you—your scorn both for things ethical and emotional—would, if I were your wife, become hateful to me; and your close acquaintance with feminine psychology and the art of love-making, would either be dangerous to me, or, as recalling past times, unpleasant at the least. And you, you would have to become insincere; to gain a wife, you would necessarily lose a friend: and surely a friend is worth more. . . ."

He walked along in silence, listening to me.

"And besides," I concluded, "let me tell you that you have come too late. A year ago, at the time when you never would treat me but as a friend, it would have been possible.

Then I was not unfrequently vexed with you, calling you (I remember) a boarding school miss, when you extolled friendship and poured your love-theory into my ears. To-day I am not for love any more. Not because Fate has dealt me any crushing blow. Nothing of the sort; but merely because it has all been most fearfully boring to me. And at present I am taking my revenge for it upon you, in the proverbial phrase: 'Let us remain friends.' "

I had quickened my pace. Wiazewski said not a word. I felt as if I was hastening towards a dark chasm which ever drew back before me, fleeing as I advanced. . . . I want all to be over—to lie there, at the bottom of that murky chasm; and, do what I may, I cannot arrive at the brink. And my teeth are clenched with pain.

"If you knew how madly I love the exceeding sweetness of his mouth!" The words flashed then through my mind: a reminiscence of the far-off, far-off Past!

"I cannot understand you in the least. Never, never, should I have acted so in your place."

"Well, Gina, it is over. Tell me now what

remedy you would advise me to take. How
do you yourself manage to bear life? To remain passive, doing nothing—that were surely
impossible. Work? But work is of no avail.
Unless something happens to rescue me, I
shall have to leave the office; I fear I am about
to go mad. . . . Are you still interested in
art? You paint very little now; I cannot
make out why."

Gina shook her head with a drowsy air. "I
always preferred Life to Art."

"Why," I said, noticing that she was in
evening dress, "you are going out to-night!"
The thought of staying by myself all the evening made me shudder. At the same time, I
felt my cheeks colouring, for I feared there
was a mortification in store for me which I
could not understand. "I trust you will tell
me quite frankly."

For a few seconds she knit her brows and
reflected. Then, "I think," she said, "that it
will not be impossible. . . . I have for a long
time wished to make you the proposal; but, in
such a matter, one cannot be too cautious. . . .
Yet, after all, we too have something in common. And I have learned to know you."

Abruptly she came to a decision.

"Then—yes, I can recommend something to you. If you hold out, it is only by its means."

"Give it me, quick!"

"Wait a little. I must in the first place demand of you to keep this a profound secret. I hide nothing else that I do: yet this I hide. Secondly: it is something that, for effects and surroundings' sake, we do in conclave. I shall take you there."

We went.

Radlowski came to open the door. When he saw me, he was taken aback, though he tried to carry it off under a show of courtesy.

"We have a neophyte here," Gina explained.

But the explanation rather increased than removed his trouble, though he at once pretended lively satisfaction. He said aside to Gina: "But something must be done: Emma is here."

Gina laughed. "Oh, all the better! If you have nothing but that to make you uneasy!"

Radlowski was now more at ease. He ushered us into his bedchamber, beyond the studio, and left us there together. Now and then we could hear a confused sound of talk-

ing, though the voices were low, in the next
room.

"And Emma, who is she?" I asked.

"Oh, a most beautiful woman, though not
exactly admissible into society. One of the
celebrated *étoiles* of beauty, formerly a model
of Radlowski's."

Gina, picking up a small phial from the
toilet table, took some of the contents herself,
and then gave me directions how the narcotic
was to be taken.

We went into the studio, where a wealth of
carpets, hangings, bits of tapestry, and wide
low Ottomans was scattered about. Nothing
here revealed the artistic disorder of the
typical *atelier*. In a corner, however, there
stood an easel, with a half-finished canvas—a
portrait; and several paintings hung from the
walls.

By the delicate radiance of several glass and
paper patterns of artistic design, I perceived
some men and women, who all rose to greet
us as we came in.

Emma I recognized at the first glance. She
got up and walked slowly towards Gina, looking all the time straight at us, out of wonderfully bright and unnaturally dilated pupils.

She wore what was not so much a dress as a veil, beneath whose light clinging folds, of a steely blue tint, the shape of her body, not covered by any other garment, was discerni-ble; and a broad Venetian girdle, gold-wrought and ponderous, dangled from the wide hips round which it passed.

Many a fair woman have I seen in my life; but, at her sight, I overflowed with admira-tion. As soon as I beheld her, I had a desire to laugh aloud, and kneel down, and thank her for that she was so marvellously fair.

All that had hitherto fascinated me now seemed to be effete and colourless. I would never have believed that any being so majesti-cal, so like a classical antique, so royally more than beautiful, could exist in the real world. All there was of pure nature in her was— that she *lived;* the rest appeared like a master-piece of painting, of sculpture, of poetry. She was indeed fairer than anything in nature— whether in the azure heavens, or in the mead-ows, or in the forests—fairer than a Midsum-mer night!

She kissed Gina as she went forward to wel-come her. To me she gave her hand only, with a courteous but frigid mien. Her eyes, looking into mine, expressed distrust and scrutiny, though she strove to appear icily serene.

The other woman present belonged without question to "good society"; a pleasant, handsome, dreamy blonde. Radlowski, when he introduced us to each other, artfully found means to avoid uttering her name. She was one of the *irréprochables,* come here incognito. All the men were already known to me by name: two painters, a few literary men, and a poet. Like Emma, they too had unnaturally dilated pupils; Radlowski, Gina, and the irreproachable unknown lady were all alike in this respect.

On making acquaintance with these people, I remarked, not without a pleasant surprise, that all the collars were immaculate, and none turned down; that not one tie was eccentric, not one head of hair superabundant. On the contrary, their dress was in good taste, their behaviour unaffected, their bearing quietly refined. Seen in the midst of this company, Emma was a far greater anachronism—twice as striking, twice as fantastic.

They all speak under their breath; no one contradicts, no one is excited. There is no general conversation, only a few utterances

here and there. They talk neither of literature, nor of painting; life, and the present
day, is all they speak of. They hold discourse
about frivolous or ordinary matters, with
elaborate elegance; and their fashion of taking things, their tone and temper, shows at
once what manner of men they are. They are
of those who have now left behind them the
Past—the stress and storm of finally triumphant Decadentism—and have arrived at
some sort of fragmentary synthesis, which they
have set up as their standard. Their mental
equilibrium has bestowed upon them an amazing excellence of form, a philosophical calm
in their way of looking upon the world, and
an ecstatic cult of life, which, from their
standpoint, becomes all but synonymous with
the Beautiful. They are all characterized by
great enlightenment, mental distinction, contempt for all unsightly mediocrity, picturesque in their life, and a moderation inex-
pressibly artistic and reposeful—something
like the Greek soul.

One of the painters exclaimed: "I should
like to remind Emma of the promise she made
us last night, which was so gratifying to us
all."

"Ah, yes: we are all expectant."

"Emma is something of a *littérateur,* and writes poetry," a slender fair-haired young man beside me explained.

An exception to the universal custom took place. She made no bashful excuses.

"As you like," she said.

With exquisite grace in every movement, she rose from the sofa, and traversed the studio slowly, that we might feast our enchanted eyes on the spectacle of that fairy-like beauty.

Enamoured, not unlike Narcissus, of her own goodly form, and radiant with her lofty queen-like head, her shoulders moulded as perfectly as a Greek statue, her cream-hued limbs just visible beneath the clinging tissue that she wore—she came to a standstill opposite me. With a motion as harmoniously entrancing as a strain of music, she adjusted the golden fillet on her superbly chiselled Pagan brow, and began her recitation:

She is in love, the Ice-Queen,—charmed and spell-bound;
Strings of cold pearls fall from her iced cascades;
Flowers in her frozen cisterns weirdly blossom;
Flowers in her chilly grottoes flame like gold.

I have this night guessed the stars' Runic riddle: . . .
There, on the verdant banks of Life,—alas!
Some one hath rent in twain the shroud sepulchral. . . .
Under that shroud sepulchral Sleep lies dead.

Why should I yearn impatient for the morning,
Since it is writ that I expire at dawn?
Oh,—for my heart distraught still loves Life madly,—
I will my true love call to me to-day!

"Come to me, dear one! greet me, but in silence,
Lest thou shouldst wake sad Memory's sleeping ghosts;
Quietly let them down, the ice-cold curtains:
Quietly draw the silken veils aside.

"Come to my tent, though dark it is around us:
Fear not; the stars are twinkling soft above;
(Fain would my wings of silver soar to join them!):
Cover thine eyes, love, from the dread black night!

"Wilt thou two clusters—grapes with warm blood swell-
          ing?
Lay twixt my breasts, O lay thy golden head!
Me let thine arms, mighty with youth's keen transport,
Clasp in embraces like the serpent's coil.

"Here is no skiey vault unfathomable;
Here are no stars that gleam athwart the blue.—
They are a silken tent, my silky tresses;
Stars, too, shine bright:—naught but mine eyes are they!

"Take thou my blood, take all that is my being:
Give me my memories, my sleep of yore!—
I had a dream that froze my founts of gladness—
I had a dream, . . . dim ghosts with muffled sobs!

"Dreams are but dreams!—Seest thou the sun's red circle;
Huge, tinged with gore o' the early dawn?—Thy lips,—
Oh, how I love them—they are crimson roses,
Roses of kingly purple, . . . and are mine!

"Broken my wings are: at thy feet I lay them
(Soaring aloft i' the airy void, they broke):
Oh, how I love thee! Thou'rt a golden garland
Glinting resplendent in my silky hair!"

The recitation over, she waved us a salute, and a gold bracelet flashed above the elbow of her bare arm. Then she sank on to the nearest sofa, covered with carpeting of a rich pattern. She received no thanks, nor did she expect any. There she lay, her hands clasped beneath her head, and the black diamonds of her eyes gazing steadfastly up to the ceiling.

"Oh, what heavenly bliss I am beginning to feel now!" was the thought that flashed upon me all at once.

Yes, the narcotic was acting already. Everything in me that was evil, or pained, or imperfect, had vanished away. I was filled

with light—a chilly splendour, supremely
contemptuous of all things, supremely bliss-
ful.

The chill had spread around me. There
was,—in the wide-open, quiescent eyes of all
those men, gazing as in a hypnotic trance
upon the miracle of female beauty which they
beheld,—the uncanny greenish light which
certain gases in slow combustion give out.
We were in an atmosphere of superhuman
delight; a delight that was not earthly; the
sempiternally fascinating delight of Non-
Existence.

There was a hearkening to the silence, and
a listening with riveted and petrified attention. The least little murmur of life gave
pain. No one was allowed into the studio;
black coffee was poured out by Radlowski
and Gina, and brought to each of us by them.
And soft and low fell slowly from our lips
words as of silken tissue, containing thoughts
of delicate essence, recondite and shrouded in
mystery.

The unknown blonde was saying to Emma:

"At such moments as these, I never give one
thought to my lover. . . . I wish to feel no
love for him, in order that I may dream of

Love itself. . . . I see a land such as on earth
there is none: where a Not-sun shines, and
where Not-flowers have fragrance! A vision!
. . . I behold a lover who is not of the earth,
and him alone I love. . . . In a vision. . . .
In my slumbers!"

"There is nothing in the world," said
Emma, "so beautiful as that which is not in it.
. . . Oh, how sweet is the craving after the
love that is nowhere to be found!"

We were all experiencing an extraordinary
and ecstatic glow: and in our state nothing
appeared too naïve or too *exalté*.

I felt full of kindly inclination towards
these people, and of deep gratitude as well,
because they were all in such harmony with
one another. It was almost pure ideal friendship, based on community of admirations and
disdains, and mutually uniting all those of the
same caste: the cool and egotistical friendship
which one demigod may feel for another.

The slenderly built young man whom I
have mentioned leant forward to me:

"Pray tell me something of love."

"Love? I know one kind only."

"And what is that?"

"The fanatical, the Pagan love of Self."

I clasped my hands, and rested my head upon them. Looking forth into that infinite distance where all is rigid, where no motion is possible, and partly unconscious of what I was saying, I spoke thus:

"Oh! how I love myself in all my manifestations! In all my loves and abhorrences; in all my dreamings and scornings; in all those most mournful victories of my own unconquerable strength!—Ah! how willingly would I die this very night, this wonderful night of the blossoming and perishing of my desires!"

From one instant to the next, my feelings were growing stranger and stranger. Something akin to dread was now taking hold upon me. Somewhere—far, far away, as it were down at the very bottom of the gulf of Life,—I heard a carriage clatter past, and a shudder of unutterable dismay then shook me. Unwittingly, I drew closer to my next neighbour. . . . Presently, I was aware of the soothing, almost spiritual caress of some one's cool white hand, passing over my forehead. As I felt it stroke me so gently, my alarms were dispelled; and again I was steeped in that phosphorescent zodiacal luminosity, as of gases in slow combustion.

And now it returned, that vision, that majestic long-forgotten vision. Once more I saw around me the endless stretches of the icy plains. The sun was not seen in the jet-black sky; and above the horizon rose the cold greenish glimmer of the Northern Lights. And lo, those cold dead dreams of mine had come to life again!

There is no more any Ego of mine. . . . I am beyond existence and beyond nothingness—in that world wherein dies the immemorial conflict between dream and vigil, where Wrong, robed in her queenly purple, is no longer shadowed by Vengeance, attired in pallid green; where stony Hatred no longer hugs in her fierce embrace the weeping god of love; where the marble statue of Pride no more does homage to the grim spectre, Fear; wherein there are no more wretched victories, nor the portentous delights of worshipping Self and the Power of Self!

And I am in such bliss—bliss so celestial, so divine!

That?—Oh, *that*? . . . It has passed away. Only . . . from time to time . . .

Yes, from time to time, I cast away all

traces of kisses in the Past—put aside my
wreath of purple velvet flowers—and go,
walking tranquilly and slowly, by the cold
light of the moon, to kneel at the grave where
my dreams lie buried, and press my brow to
the base of the tombstone that covers them,
. . . and muse.

Once, I hung up a wreath of snow-white
lilies there; now, I do so no more. I never
carry any flowers to that tomb now.

Nor do I ever strive to roll away the grey
stone from the sepulchre—that stone, with its
black fretwork of ferns graven upon it of old.

Then I go home, and again array myself in
my purple velvet flowers. . . .

Fragrance, beyond words, wild and fatal
perfume of withered roses! Sweet, most
sweet and ardent lips—lips now lost for ever!
. . . Ah, that houri, with arms like pale dead
gold!

All this—I can no longer say whether it
was a dream or not. . . .

Ah! but what is this? Have the cool white
lilies blossomed once again in my deserted
garden?

A dream!—A dream!

That hand, of pure white tint,
Full fain a bell would swing
That nevermore may ring,
For the long rift within't.

But why then am I so immensely, so divine-ly happy?

Those eyes, dim, sweet, and sad, of him who once was mine!—I can no longer say whether it was all a dream, or not. My ice-plains once more, my ice-plains!—No—before these—still farther back! . . . still farther! An-other, and a far different, sweet smell: a fresh delicious perfume—of meadows in flower, of willow catkins, of the lilacs in blossom.—Yel-low marigolds! (O heavens, those strange far-off memories!) . . . O sunshine, O green fields, O adorable bygone days! . . . O my childhood!

Tears flow in torrents—tears for the sun-shine, for life, for happiness.—Do not wipe my eyes, for they are dropping pearls! Why, brush those pearls away?

That hand, of pure white tint,
Oh, let it never swing
The bell which cannot ring
For the deep rift that's in't.

I awoke long after daybreak.

Gina was bending over me.

"Let us leave the place," she said; "you are a little shaken. A usual thing the first time. You must accustom yourself."

A tall woman, draped from head to foot in a long mantle of white fur, was waiting for us. Her complexion was of a muddy yellowish hue; her eyes were dull and sodden. It took me more than one glance to make sure who she was.

We were accompanied to the carriage by a grey-haired gentleman whom—so far as I could remember—I had never seen before.

I put up my hands to my eyes, unwilling now to look upon the world any more.

And with this my canticle of love comes to an end.

I had asked Smilowicz to let the Professor know I was going to call upon him: and I have been there to-day.

What a curious feeling I had in beholding once more those solemn-looking apartments, lined all round with books up to the very ceiling and the same beautiful old man, now a little older!

He welcomed me with joy.

"My prodigal daughter," he said, "is ever so much dearer to me now than before!"

To have kept complete silence about the rupture which had taken place, would not have satisfied his kindness.

"You must not fancy I am quite disinterested in wishing you back again," he said. "I have something special in view."

"What may that be, Professor?"

"I have just received permission from the Russian Government to publish a scientific journal, and it has confirmed me in my status as editor. As my secretary, you would be useful, and I ask you to accept the position."

"I should do so with pleasure, but my occupation prevents me."

"Your office? You will give it up: it is no fitting situation for you. I have been thinking it over: this is just what will serve most to bring your abilities into full play. You will have to do the 'Intelligence' columns, make summaries, and write translations—at first. And it will be necessary to read very, very much. I have by me a great number of new and highly interesting works, which I must show you.—Well, what do you say?"

I said yes.

During our conversation, I was under the same impression that I had, when I went to see Mme. Smilowicz. I was no longer 'up-to-date,' for I had long given up reading.—Obojanski talked at length to me about various changes that had latterly taken place in his field of science.

Those last years had been lost for me. My abandonment of the "Ice-plains" had cost me dear. I had learned nothing by having become acquainted with Life; I was not capable of forming any synthetic views about it. The more we know of it, the less is it possible to comprehend it in any systematized generalization.—Everything in Life contradicts everything else: Science is by far more consistent.

"But," Obojanski asked, "to what am I to ascribe your return?"

"To Smilowicz."

"I don't mean that. There must have been something deeper down—some change in your mind and views, eh?"

He no doubt expected to hear some romantic phrases about the barrenness of life spent as in those years, and of its failure to give me happiness.

Instead of which, I made him this unforeseen reply:

"Well, on the whole, it is because I prefer to return to you whom I have left, rather than to the Church!"

And Obojanski eyed me in bewilderment.

THE END.

*A Selection from the
Catalogue of*

G. P. PUTNAM'S SONS

**Complete Catalogues sent
on application**

The
Rose of Jericho

By

Ruth Holt Boucicault

It is a remarkable fact that stories
of the stage seldom reflect its ro-
mance and glamour. This story has
caught both and at the same time is
faithful to that mimic world. We
have here lifelike character por-
trayal, a heroine of courage and fas-
cination, and that struggle against
odds, new and unusual, which is
indispensable to any vital story.

G. P. Putnam's Sons

New York   London

The Comédienne

By

Wladyslaw Reymont

"THE COMÉDIENNE" is the tale of a Polish girl who rebels against her drab existence in a remote hamlet, and joins a company of provincial players. Against the colorful background of this theatrical life her tragic story is woven.

The character and development of this strange young Slavic woman and the settings and personalities of her environment are described with graphic strength by Wladyslaw Reymont.

G. P. Putnam's Sons

New York   London

THE STRANGENESS OF NOEL CARTON

By

WILLIAM CAINE

Noel Carton, driven to desperation by his vulgar little wife who, in buying his position, is forced to accept him with it, determines to bury himself in the writing of a novel, in the vain hope of forgetting. At the same time he elects to keep a secret journal. In his novel he subconsciously draws the portraits of the living people surrounding him.

How this novel becomes inextricably entangled with his own journal is the basis for this extraordinarily original story which leads to an astounding climax.

G. P. PUTNAM'S SONS

New York   London

Lightning Source UK Ltd.
Milton Keynes UK
01 March 2010

150795UK00006B/66/A